new Casseroles

THE AUSTRALIAN
Women's Weekly

Thinking about casseroles, I am always reminded of the homely smell that fills the house, the succulent slow-cooked meat falling off the bone and the creamy mashes and bakes that accompany them. We all so enjoyed putting this book together — the aromas and flavours of our casseroles were almost as good as the memories.

Pamela Clark

Food Director

contents

casserole basics

slow cooker

As a guide, recipes where long, slow oven or cook-top cooking is specified are suitable for a slow cooker.

Before you begin, it is important to thoroughly read the manufacturer's instructions. Always follow all safety precautions.

Refer to the recipe booklet provided by the manufacturer to work out the cooking time for the recipes you select from this book.

Always cover a slow cooker with its lid; do not lift the lid too often during cooking in order to maintain heat.

Slow cookers do not allow food to reach a high temperature; the food is meant to be cooked over a long period of time — up to about 8 hours.

Coating the meat in flour and browning it before adding it to the slow cooker helps keep the meat tender and locks in the juices of the meat.

If your casserole has too much liquid, turn the slow cooker onto the highest setting and cook, uncovered, until some of the liquid has evaporated.

microwave

We haven't tested any of these recipes in the microwave, but there are many parts of these recipes that would be suitable for microwave cooking. Most casseroles can be cooked in the microwave oven, but we prefer the longer, slower cooking methods.

It's important to follow the manufacturer's instructions when using your microwave, and always follow all safety precautions.

A combination of convection and microwave cooking will give good results.

pressure cooker

Many of our recipes can be adapted to cook in a pressure cooker; check the note at the end of each recipe. We have said "not suitable" when casseroles cook in about 30 to 40 minutes.

Before you begin, it is important to thoroughly read the manufacturer's instructions. Always follow all safety precautions.

You may need to refer to the recipe booklet provided by the manufacturer to work out the cooking time for the recipes you select from this book.

Cut the meat into even-sized pieces to ensure even cooking.

Recipes with a high liquid content usually work best for pressure cookers.

You should never fill the pressure cooker more than two-thirds full.

As a rule, cooking time can be reduced to about a third. For example, if a casserole is cooked in the oven for 1 hour, it could be expected to cook in a pressure cooker in about 20 minutes.

Thicken with cornflour, etc., and add herbs and green vegetables after the meat or chicken is tender, or just before serving. Simply remove the lid and use the pressure cooker like a saucepan.

beef and eggplant bake with polenta crust

PREPARATION TIME 20 MINUTES (PLUS STANDING TIME) **COOKING TIME** 1 HOUR 20 MINUTES **SERVES** 6

2 medium eggplants (600g), sliced thickly

2 tablespoons coarse cooking salt

1 tablespoon olive oil

1 medium brown onion (150g), chopped coarsely

1 medium red capsicum (200g), chopped coarsely

1 clove garlic, crushed

500g beef mince

2 tablespoons tomato paste

½ cup (125ml) dry red wine

400g can whole tomatoes

1 cup firmly packed fresh basil leaves

1 tablespoon fresh oregano leaves

2 cups (500ml) chicken stock

2 cups (500ml) milk

1 cup (170g) polenta

1½ cups (150g) coarsely grated mozzarella cheese

Have you ever eaten eggplant that's disagreeably bitter? It's easy to avoid this taste by simply treating the eggplant to a process known as disgorging. Cut the eggplant, place in a colander, sprinkle all over with salt then stand for at least half an hour. The salt will turn slightly brown as it absorbs the bitter liquid. Rinse eggplant pieces under cold water then pat dry with absorbent paper.

1 Place eggplant in colander, sprinkle all over with salt; stand 30 minutes. Rinse eggplant; drain on absorbent paper.

2 Meanwhile, heat oil in medium frying pan; cook onion, capsicum and garlic, stirring, until onion softens. Add beef; cook, stirring, until beef changes colour. Add paste; cook, stirring, 2 minutes. Add wine; cook, stirring, 5 minutes. Add undrained tomatoes; bring to a boil. Reduce heat; simmer, uncovered, stirring occasionally, about 15 minutes or until liquid is almost evaporated. Chop about a quarter of the basil leaves coarsely; stir into sauce with oregano.

3 Preheat oven to moderately hot.

4 Cook eggplant on heated oiled grill plate (or grill or barbecue) until just browned.

5 Meanwhile, combine stock and milk in medium saucepan; bring to a boil. Gradually add polenta, stirring constantly. Reduce heat; simmer, stirring, about 10 minutes or until polenta thickens.

6 Arrange half of the eggplant in shallow 3-litre (12-cup) baking dish; top with half of the beef mixture. Top with remaining eggplant then remaining beef mixture and remaining basil. Spread polenta over basil; sprinkle with cheese. Cook, uncovered, in moderately hot oven about 20 minutes or until top is browned lightly. Stand 10 minutes before serving with a mixed green salad, if desired.

PER SERVING	
total fat	19.9g
saturated fat	8.7g
kilojoules	1877
calories	449
carbohydrates	32g
protein	32.3g
fibre	4.7g

SLOW COOKER **NOT SUITABLE**   PRESSURE COOKER **NOT SUITABLE**   FREEZE **NOT SUITABLE**

beef, barley and mushroom stew with parsnip mash

PREPARATION TIME 35 MINUTES **COOKING TIME** 2 HOURS 20 MINUTES **SERVES** 4

PARSNIP MASH Boil, steam or microwave 1kg coarsely chopped parsnip until tender; drain. Mash parsnip in medium bowl with ¾ cup hot milk until smooth; stir in 2 crushed cloves garlic and 40g softened butter.

1kg beef chuck steak, diced into 3cm pieces

¼ cup (35g) plain flour

2 tablespoons olive oil

20g butter

2 medium brown onions (300g), chopped finely

3 cloves garlic, crushed

1 medium carrot (120g), chopped finely

1 trimmed celery stalk (100g), chopped finely

4 sprigs fresh thyme

1 sprig fresh rosemary

1 bay leaf

½ cup (100g) pearl barley

2 cups (500ml) beef stock

½ cup (125ml) dry white wine

2 cups (500ml) water

200g swiss brown mushrooms, quartered

200g button mushrooms, quartered

1 Preheat oven to moderately slow.
2 Coat beef in flour; shake off excess. Heat oil in large flameproof casserole dish; cook beef, in batches, until browned all over.
3 Melt butter in same dish; cook onion, garlic, carrot, celery and herbs, stirring, until vegetables soften. Add barley, stock, wine and the water; bring to a boil. Return beef to dish, cover; cook in moderately slow oven 1½ hours.
4 Stir in mushrooms; cook, uncovered, in moderately slow oven about 30 minutes or until beef and mushrooms are tender.
5 Meanwhile, make parsnip mash.
6 Serve stew with mash sprinkled with fresh thyme, if desired.

PER SERVING (incl. mash)	
total fat	35.1g
saturated fat	14.7g
kilojoules	3390
calories	811
carbohydrates	52.7g
protein	66.1g
fibre	13.7g

SLOW COOKER SUITABLE   PRESSURE COOKER SUITABLE UP TO STEP 4   FREEZE SUITABLE

veal with red wine and balsamic vinegar

PREPARATION TIME 25 MINUTES **COOKING TIME** 2 HOURS **SERVES** 4

Ask your butcher to dice the veal shoulder for you.

¼ cup (60ml) olive oil

1kg diced veal shoulder

10 pickling onions (400g), halved

1 medium carrot (120g), chopped finely

1 trimmed celery stalk (100g), chopped finely

2 cloves garlic, chopped finely

4 bacon rashers (280g), rind removed, chopped coarsely

¼ cup (60ml) balsamic vinegar

2 tablespoons tomato paste

200g mushrooms, quartered

425g can diced tomatoes

1 cup (250ml) dry red wine

1 cup (250ml) beef stock

2 tablespoons coarsely chopped fresh garlic chives

1 Preheat oven to moderately slow.
2 Heat 2 tablespoons of the oil in large flameproof casserole dish; cook veal, in batches, until browned all over.
3 Heat remaining oil in same dish; cook onion, carrot, celery, garlic and bacon, stirring, until vegetables soften. Add vinegar and paste; cook, uncovered, 2 minutes.
4 Add mushrooms, undrained tomatoes, wine and stock; bring to a boil. Boil, uncovered, 5 minutes. Return veal to dish, cover; cook in moderately slow oven about 1½ hours or until veal is tender. Stir in chives.
5 Meanwhile, make creamy garlic mash; serve with veal.

CREAMY GARLIC MASH
Place 1kg coarsely chopped potato, 3 cups milk and 1 peeled garlic clove in medium saucepan; bring to a boil. Reduce heat; simmer, partially covered, about 15 minutes or until potato is soft. Discard garlic. Strain potato over medium jug; reserve ⅔ cup of the milk. Transfer potato to large bowl; mash with reserved milk and 40g of softened butter until smooth.

PER SERVING (incl. mash)	
total fat	25.5g
saturated fat	5.6g
kilojoules	2495
calories	597
carbohydrates	11.2g
protein	69.5g
fibre	5.6g

SLOW COOKER SUITABLE   PRESSURE COOKER SUITABLE   FREEZE SUITABLE

veal with artichokes, olives and lemon

PREPARATION TIME 40 MINUTES   **COOKING TIME** 2 HOURS 25 MINUTES   **SERVES** 6

Penne rigate is one of the best all-rounders when choosing a pasta to serve as an accompaniment to a saucy main course. Short, hardy and hollow, it's got just the right amount of "chew" and its cavity helps secret away a burst of sauce. As with all ridged pastas, the lengthways grooves capture and hold the dish's sauce, as opposed to the smooth-surfaced penne lisce.

1 medium unpeeled lemon (140g), chopped coarsely

4 medium globe artichokes (800g)

1.2kg diced veal neck

¼ cup (35g) plain flour

50g butter

¼ cup (60ml) olive oil

1 medium brown onion (150g), chopped finely

1 medium carrot (120g), chopped finely

2 cloves garlic, chopped finely

2 sprigs fresh marjoram

2 sprigs fresh oregano

1 cup (250ml) dry white wine

2 cups (500ml) chicken stock

1 cup (150g) seeded kalamata olives

2 teaspoons finely grated lemon rind

2 tablespoons lemon juice

2 tablespoons fresh oregano leaves

1 medium lemon (140g), cut into six wedges

1 Place chopped lemon in large bowl half-filled with cold water. Discard outer leaves from artichokes; cut tips from remaining leaves. Trim then peel stalks. Quarter artichokes lengthways; using teaspoon, remove and discard chokes. Place in lemon water.
2 Preheat oven to moderately slow.
3 Coat veal in flour; shake off excess. Heat butter and 2 tablespoons of the oil in large flameproof casserole dish; cook veal, in batches, until browned all over.
4 Heat remaining oil in same dish; cook onion, carrot, garlic, marjoram and oregano sprigs, stirring, until vegetables soften. Add wine; bring to a boil. Return veal to dish with stock, cover; cook in moderately slow oven 1 hour.
5 Add artichokes; cook in moderately slow oven 30 minutes. Uncover; cook about 30 minutes or until veal is tender. Stir in olives, rind and juice. Divide among serving plates; top with oregano leaves. Serve with lemon wedges and penne, if desired.

PER SERVING	
total fat	21.6g
saturated fat	7.4g
kilojoules	2040
calories	488
carbohydrates	14.6g
protein	50.2g
fibre	3.4g

SLOW COOKER SUITABLE   PRESSURE COOKER SUITABLE UP TO STEP 5   FREEZE SUITABLE

braised lamb shanks with white bean puree

PREPARATION TIME 40 MINUTES **COOKING TIME** 2 HOURS 30 MINUTES **SERVES** 4

Many varieties of already-cooked white beans are available canned, among them cannellini, butter and haricot beans; any of these are suitable for this puree.

1 tablespoon olive oil

8 french-trimmed lamb shanks (2kg)

1 large red onion (300g), chopped coarsely

2 cloves garlic, crushed

1 cup (250ml) chicken stock

2 cups (500ml) water

400g can diced tomatoes

1 tablespoon fresh rosemary leaves

4 anchovy fillets, drained, chopped coarsely

2 large red capsicums (700g)

2 large green capsicums (700g)

WHITE BEAN PUREE

20g butter

1 small brown onion (80g), chopped finely

1 clove garlic, crushed

¼ cup (60ml) dry white wine

¾ cup (180ml) chicken stock

2 x 400g cans white beans, rinsed, drained

2 tablespoons cream

1 Heat oil in large deep saucepan; cook lamb, in batches, until browned all over.

2 Cook onion and garlic in same pan, stirring, until onion softens. Add stock, the water, undrained tomatoes, rosemary and anchovy; bring to a boil. Return lamb to pan, reduce heat; simmer, covered, 1 hour, stirring occasionally. Uncover; simmer about 45 minutes or until lamb is tender.

3 Meanwhile, quarter capsicums; discard seeds and membranes. Roast under hot grill or in very hot oven, skin-side up, until skin blisters and blackens. Cover capsicum pieces with plastic wrap or paper for 5 minutes; peel away skin, slice thickly.

4 Meanwhile, make white bean puree.

5 Add capsicum to lamb; cook, uncovered, 5 minutes. Serve lamb on white bean puree.

WHITE BEAN PUREE Melt butter in medium frying pan; cook onion and garlic, stirring, until onions softens. Add wine; cook, stirring, until liquid is reduced by half. Add stock and beans; bring to a boil. Reduce heat; simmer, uncovered, about 10 minutes or until liquid is almost evaporated. Blend or process bean mixture and cream until smooth.

PER SERVING	
total fat	18.8g
saturated fat	8.4g
kilojoules	2312
calories	553
carbohydrates	21g
protein	72.1g
fibre	8.6g

SLOW COOKER SUITABLE UP TO STEP 3   PRESSURE COOKER SUITABLE UP TO STEP 3   FREEZE LAMB SUITABLE

rogan josh

PREPARATION TIME 20 MINUTES   **COOKING TIME** 2 HOURS   **SERVES** 4

CUCUMBER RAITA
Served with meat curries such as this rogan josh, raita not only introduces different flavours to a meal but also tempers the spiciness of the dish. Combine 1 cup thick "country-style" yogurt, 1 finely chopped seeded lebanese cucumber and 1 tablespoon finely chopped fresh mint in a small bowl with salt, pepper and ground cumin to taste.

2 teaspoons ground cardamom

2 teaspoons ground cumin

2 teaspoons ground coriander

1kg boned leg of lamb, trimmed, diced into 3cm pieces

20g butter

2 tablespoons vegetable oil

2 medium brown onions (300g), sliced thinly

4cm piece fresh ginger (20g), grated

4 cloves garlic, crushed

2 teaspoons sweet paprika

½ teaspoon cayenne pepper

½ cup (125ml) beef stock

425g can crushed tomatoes

2 bay leaves

2 cinnamon sticks

200g yogurt

¾ cup (110g) toasted slivered almonds

1 fresh long red chilli, sliced thinly

1 Combine cardamom, cumin and coriander in medium bowl, add lamb; toss lamb to coat in spice mixture.
2 Heat butter and half of the oil in large deep saucepan; cook lamb, in batches, until browned all over.
3 Heat remaining oil in same pan; cook onion, ginger, garlic, paprika and cayenne over low heat, stirring, until onion softens.
4 Return lamb to pan with stock, undrained tomatoes, bay leaves and cinnamon. Add yogurt, 1 tablespoon at a time, stirring well between each addition; bring to a boil. Reduce heat; simmer, covered, about 1½ hours or until lamb is tender.
5 Meanwhile, make cucumber raita. Sprinkle lamb with nuts and chilli off the heat; serve with raita and, if desired, warmed naan bread.

PER SERVING (incl. raita)	
total fat	48.1g
saturated fat	15.3g
kilojoules	3219
calories	770
carbohydrates	15.7g
protein	68.9g
fibre	5.5g

SLOW COOKER **NOT SUITABLE**   PRESSURE COOKER **NOT SUITABLE**   FREEZE **SUITABLE**

braised leg of lamb with beans

PREPARATION TIME 30 MINUTES (PLUS STANDING TIME) **COOKING TIME** 2 HOURS 10 MINUTES **SERVES** 6

1 cup (200g) dried borlotti beans

6 cloves garlic, crushed

1 tablespoon coarsely chopped fresh rosemary

2 teaspoons sea salt

1 teaspoon cracked black pepper

¼ cup (60ml) olive oil

1.5kg butterflied leg of lamb

2 medium brown onions (300g), chopped coarsely

2 medium carrots (240g), chopped coarsely

2 trimmed celery stalks (200g), chopped coarsely

2 bay leaves

2 sprigs fresh rosemary

1 cup (250ml) dry white wine

2 cups (500ml) chicken stock

1 Place beans in medium bowl, cover with cold water; stand overnight, drain. Rinse under cold water; drain. Cook beans in medium saucepan of boiling water, uncovered, about 15 minutes or until beans are just tender; drain.

2 Preheat oven to moderately slow.

3 Combine garlic, chopped rosemary, salt, pepper and 1 tablespoon of the oil in small bowl. Place lamb, cut-side up, on board; rub garlic mixture into lamb. Roll lamb tightly; secure at 2cm intervals with kitchen string.

4 Heat remaining oil in large deep flameproof baking dish; cook lamb until browned all over. Remove lamb from dish.

5 Cook onion, carrot and celery in same dish, stirring, until onion softens. Add beans, bay leaves, rosemary sprigs, wine and stock; bring to a boil.

6 Return lamb to dish, cover; cook in moderately slow oven 1 hour.

7 Uncover; cook in moderately slow oven 30 minutes. Discard herbs; remove lamb from dish. Cover lamb to keep warm; stand 10 minutes before slicing thickly. Serve lamb on bean mixture, accompanied by mashed potatoes.

MASHED POTATOES Boil, steam or microwave 800g coarsely chopped potatoes until tender; drain. Mash potato with 50g softened butter and ½ cup hot cream in medium bowl until smooth.

PER SERVING (incl. mash)	
total fat	45.2g
saturated fat	20.3g
kilojoules	3306
calories	791
carbohydrates	29g
protein	61.8g
fibre	5.6g

SLOW COOKER SUITABLE   PRESSURE COOKER SUITABLE UP TO STEP 7   FREEZE SUITABLE

sweet and sour tamarind pork

PREPARATION TIME 25 MINUTES **COOKING TIME** 50 MINUTES **SERVES** 4

Also known as ka, galangal is a rhizome with a hot ginger-citrusy flavour that is used similarly to ginger and garlic as a seasoning and as an ingredient. Sometimes known as Thai, Siamese or Laos ginger, it also comes in a powdered form called laos. Fresh ginger can be substituted for fresh galangal but the flavour of the dish will not be exactly the same.

2 tablespoons peanut oil

4 pork forequarter chops (1kg)

1 tablespoon chinese cooking wine

1 cup (250ml) chicken stock

⅓ cup (80ml) tamarind concentrate

¼ cup (60ml) soy sauce

¼ cup (65g) grated palm sugar

1 medium red capsicum (200g), sliced thickly

1 medium green capsicum (200g), sliced thickly

1 medium red onion (170g), sliced thickly

3 green onions, sliced thickly

AROMATIC PASTE

4cm piece fresh galangal (20g), chopped finely

20cm stick fresh lemon grass (40g), chopped finely

2 cloves garlic, quartered

2 shallots (50g), chopped coarsely

1 tablespoon sambal oelek

1 Preheat oven to slow.
2 Blend or process ingredients for aromatic paste until mixture becomes a thick coarse puree.
3 Heat half of the oil in large deep flameproof baking dish; cook pork, in batches, until browned both sides.
4 Heat remaining oil in same dish; cook aromatic paste, stirring, until fragrant. Return pork to dish with wine, stock, tamarind, soy, sugar, capsicums and red onion; bring to a boil. Cover; cook in slow oven 25 minutes, turning pork once halfway through cooking time.
5 Add green onion; cook, covered, in slow oven about 10 minutes or until green onion is tender. Serve with steamed rice, if desired.

PER SERVING	
total fat	31.8g
saturated fat	9.4g
kilojoules	2462
calories	589
carbohydrates	26.3g
protein	42g
fibre	2.4g

SLOW COOKER NOT SUITABLE   PRESSURE COOKER NOT SUITABLE   FREEZE NOT SUITABLE

braised pork with pears and cider

PREPARATION TIME 10 MINUTES **COOKING TIME** 2 HOURS 15 MINUTES **SERVES** 4

2 tablespoons olive oil

1kg piece pork neck

3cm piece fresh ginger (15g), sliced thinly

2 cloves garlic, sliced thinly

½ teaspoon ground fennel

3 cups (750ml) sweet cider

2 cups (500ml) chicken stock

2 large pears (660g), peeled, cut into thick wedges

½ cup coarsely chopped fresh flat-leaf parsley

1 Preheat oven to moderately slow.
2 Heat oil in large flameproof casserole dish; cook pork until browned all over. Remove from dish.
3 Cook ginger and garlic in same dish, stirring, until fragrant. Add fennel; cook, stirring, 1 minute. Add cider and stock; bring to a boil. Return pork to dish, cover; cook in moderately slow oven 1 hour. Uncover; cook in moderately slow oven 30 minutes. Add pear; cook, uncovered, about 30 minutes or until pear is tender. Remove pork, cover, stand 5 minutes before slicing thickly. Stir parsley into braising liquid.
4 Serve pork with braising liquid and steamed broccolini, if desired.

A cross between broccoli and Chinese kale, broccolini is milder and sweeter than broccoli. Each long stem is topped by a loose floret that closely resembles broccoli; from floret to stem, broccolini is completely edible.

PER SERVING	
total fat	29.8g
saturated fat	8.3g
kilojoules	2805
calories	671
carbohydrates	34.7g
protein	55.1g
fibre	3.5g

SLOW COOKER **SUITABLE**   PRESSURE COOKER **SUITABLE**   FREEZE **SUITABLE**

chipotle pork ribs with chorizo and smoked paprika

PREPARATION TIME 20 MINUTES **COOKING TIME** 2 HOURS 50 MINUTES **SERVES** 4

ROASTED CORN SALSA
Roast 3 husked corn cobs on heated oiled grill plate (or grill or barbecue) until browned all over. When corn is cool enough to handle, cut kernels from cobs. Combine corn kernels in medium bowl with 1 coarsely chopped small red onion, 1 coarsely chopped medium avocado, 250g halved cherry tomatoes, 2 tablespoons lime juice and ¼ cup chopped fresh coriander.

Chipotle chillies, also known as ahumado, are jalapeño chillies that have been dried then smoked. They are about 6cm in length, a dark brown, almost black, colour and have a deep, intense smoky flavour rather than a blast of heat. They are available from herb and spice shops as well as many gourmet delicatessens.

4 chipotle chillies

1 cup (250ml) boiling water

1.5kg pork belly ribs

1 tablespoon olive oil

1 chorizo (170g), sliced thinly

2 medium red onions (340g), chopped coarsely

1 medium red capsicum (200g), chopped coarsely

1 medium green capsicum (200g), chopped coarsely

1 teaspoon smoked paprika

4 cloves garlic, crushed

3 x 400g cans crushed tomatoes

2 medium tomatoes (300g), chopped finely

½ cup finely chopped fresh coriander

2 teaspoons finely grated lime rind

1 clove garlic, crushed, extra

1 Preheat oven to moderately slow.
2 Soak chillies in the boiling water in small heatproof bowl for 10 minutes. Discard stalks from chillies; reserve chillies and liquid.
3 Using heavy knife, separate ribs. Heat oil in large deep flameproof baking dish; cook ribs, in batches, until browned all over.
4 Cook chorizo, onion, capsicums, paprika and garlic in same dish, stirring, until onion softens. Return ribs to dish with undrained crushed tomatoes, chillies and reserved liquid. Cover; cook in moderately slow oven about 1 hour.
5 Uncover; cook in moderately slow oven about 1½ hours or until ribs are tender.
6 Meanwhile, combine chopped tomato, coriander, rind and extra garlic in small bowl. Cover; refrigerate until required.
7 Top ribs with coriander mixture; serve with roasted corn salsa and flour tortillas, if desired.

PER SERVING (incl. salsa)	
total fat	97.7g
saturated fat	30.5g
kilojoules	5300
calories	1268
carbohydrates	41.9g
protein	57.1g
fibre	15.7g

SLOW COOKER **SUITABLE UP TO STEP 6**   PRESSURE COOKER **SUITABLE UP TO STEP 5**   FREEZE **SUITABLE**

maple-syrup-flavoured pork belly with pecans

PREPARATION TIME 20 MINUTES **COOKING TIME** 1 HOUR 50 MINUTES **SERVES** 4

Ancho chillies, the most commonly used chilli in Mexico, are poblano chillies which have been dried. Having a fruity, sweet and smoky flavour, they measure about 8cm in length and are dark reddish brown in colour.

1kg boned pork belly, cut into four pieces

1 cup (250ml) pure maple syrup

3 cups (750ml) chicken stock

1 cinnamon stick

2 ancho chillies

6 whole cloves

2 cloves garlic, crushed

½ cup (125ml) soy sauce

½ cup (125ml) orange juice

1 tablespoon olive oil

750g silverbeet, trimmed, sliced thinly

½ cup (60g) coarsely chopped roasted pecans

Many cooks think pecans are only suitable used in desserts, but they are just as good in salads, stuffings and main courses. They are also great tossed in curry spices then roasted or coated in chocolate or toffee. Studies show that pecans contain the most antioxidants of any nut and about 60 per cent of their fat content are "good" monounsaturated fats.

1 Combine pork, syrup, stock, cinnamon, chillies, cloves, garlic and soy in saucepan large enough to hold pork in a single layer; bring to a boil. Reduce heat; simmer, covered, about 1½ hours or until pork is tender, turning pork every 30 minutes. Remove pork; cover to keep warm. Stir juice into braising liquid; bring to a boil. Reduce heat; simmer, uncovered, about 5 minutes or until sauce thickens slightly. Strain sauce into small bowl.

2 Meanwhile, heat oil in large saucepan; cook silverbeet, stirring, about 5 minutes or until wilted.

3 Cut each pork piece into quarters. Divide silverbeet among plates; top with pork, drizzle with sauce then sprinkle with nuts. Serve with steamed basmati and wild rice blend, if desired.

PER SERVING	
total fat	67.2g
saturated fat	18.9g
kilojoules	4080
calories	976
carbohydrates	62.3g
protein	34.7g
fibre	4.1g

SLOW COOKER **SUITABLE UP TO STEP 2**   PRESSURE COOKER **SUITABLE UP TO STEP 2**   FREEZE **SUITABLE**

pork, chicken and black-eyed bean cassoulet

PREPARATION TIME 20 MINUTES (PLUS STANDING TIME) **COOKING TIME** 2 HOURS 45 MINUTES **SERVES** 4

Also called black-eyed peas or cow peas, the small, kidney-shaped, white bean with a single black spot used here has a fairly thin skin so cooks rather faster than other legumes. A good source of protein and complex carbohydrates, beans keep their nutritional value even through lengthy storage.

Ask your butcher to remove the rind and slice the pork for you.

1 cup (200g) black-eyed beans

1 tablespoon olive oil

500g boned pork belly, rind removed, sliced thinly

8 chicken drumettes (640g)

4 thin pork sausages (320g)

1 trimmed celery stalk (100g), sliced thinly

1 medium brown onion (150g), chopped coarsely

1 small leek (200g), sliced thinly

1 teaspoon fresh thyme leaves

½ cup (125ml) dry white wine

400g can diced tomatoes

2 cups (500ml) chicken stock

3 cups (210g) stale breadcrumbs

½ cup finely chopped fresh flat-leaf parsley

50g butter, melted

1 Place beans in medium bowl, cover with cold water; stand 3 hours or overnight, drain. Rinse under cold water; drain.
2 Preheat oven to moderate.
3 Heat oil in large flameproof casserole dish; cook pork, chicken and sausages, in batches, until browned all over.
4 Cook celery, onion, leek and thyme in same dish, stirring, until onion softens. Add wine; cook, stirring, 5 minutes. Return pork, chicken and sausages to dish with undrained tomatoes, stock and beans; cook, covered in moderate oven 40 minutes.
5 Uncover; sprinkle with combined breadcrumbs, parsley and butter. Cook, uncovered, in moderate oven about 40 minutes or until meat is tender and top is lightly browned. Serve with a curly endive salad dressed with white wine vinaigrette, if desired.

PER SERVING	
total fat	65.2g
saturated fat	25.3g
kilojoules	4314
calories	1032
carbohydrates	51.3g
protein	57g
fibre	9.9g

SLOW COOKER **SUITABLE UP TO STEP 5**   PRESSURE COOKER **SUITABLE UP TO STEP 5**   FREEZE **SUITABLE**

pork cabbage rolls

PREPARATION TIME 1 HOUR **COOKING TIME** 1 HOUR 40 MINUTES **SERVES** 6

18 large cabbage leaves

½ cup (100g) uncooked white long-grain rice

250g pork mince

1 medium brown onion (150g), chopped finely

¼ cup finely chopped fresh dill

1 clove garlic, crushed

1 tablespoon tomato paste

2 teaspoons ground cumin

1 teaspoon ground coriander

1 teaspoon ground allspice

4 cloves garlic, quartered

2 medium tomatoes (300g), chopped coarsely

2 x 400g cans crushed tomatoes

¼ cup (60ml) lemon juice

Also known as pimento or Jamaican pepper; allspice is so-named because it tastes like a combination of nutmeg, cumin, clove and cinnamon. It can be purchased either as a whole, pea-sized, dark brown berry or ground into powder, and is just as good used in dessert-making and baking as in savoury dishes.

1 Discard thick stems from 15 cabbage leaves; reserve remaining leaves. Boil, steam or microwave trimmed leaves until just pliable; drain. Rinse under cold water; drain. Pat dry with absorbent paper.

2 Using hand, combine rice, pork, onion, dill, crushed garlic, paste and spices in medium bowl.

3 Place one trimmed leaf, vein-side up, on board; cut leaf in half lengthways. Place 1 rounded teaspoon of the pork mixture at stem end of each half; roll each half firmly to enclose filling. Repeat with remaining trimmed leaves.

4 Place reserved leaves in base of large saucepan. Place only enough rolls, seam-side down, in single layer, to completely cover leaves in base of saucepan. Top with quartered garlic, chopped fresh tomato then remaining rolls.

5 Pour undrained tomatoes and juice over cabbage rolls; bring to a boil. Reduce heat; simmer, covered, 1 hour. Uncover; simmer about 30 minutes or until cabbage rolls are cooked through.

6 Serve with thick greek-style yogurt flavoured with a little finely choppped preserved lemon, if desired.

PER SERVING	
total fat	3.6g
saturated fat	1.1g
kilojoules	803
calories	192
carbohydrates	24.7g
protein	14.3g
fibre	9.7g

SLOW COOKER **SUITABLE**   PRESSURE COOKER **SUITABLE**   FREEZE **NOT SUITABLE**

italian braised pork

PREPARATION TIME 25 MINUTES **COOKING TIME** 2 HOURS 50 MINUTES **SERVES** 6

An Italian style of bacon, hot pancetta is lean pork belly that is salted and cured (but not smoked) then spiced and rolled into a fat, sausage-like loaf. It is usually only used as a flavouring in pasta sauces and meat dishes except for in its place of origin, Corsica, where it is eaten on its own, like bacon.

Ask your butcher to roll and tie the pork shoulder for you.

2 tablespoons olive oil

1.5kg pork shoulder, rolled and tied

2 cloves garlic, crushed

1 medium brown onion (150g), chopped coarsely

½ small fennel bulb (100g), chopped coarsely

8 slices hot pancetta (120g), chopped coarsely

1 tablespoon tomato paste

½ cup (125ml) dry white wine

400g can whole tomatoes

1 cup (250ml) chicken stock

1 cup (250ml) water

2 sprigs fresh rosemary

2 large fennel bulbs (1kg), halved, sliced thickly

SPICE RUB

1 teaspoon fennel seeds

2 teaspoons dried oregano

½ teaspoon cayenne pepper

1 tablespoon cracked black pepper

1 tablespoon sea salt

2 teaspoons olive oil

1 Preheat oven to moderate.
2 Heat oil in large flameproof casserole dish; cook pork, uncovered, until browned all over.
3 Meanwhile, combine ingredients for spice rub in small bowl.
4 Remove pork from dish; discard all but 1 tablespoon of the oil in dish. Cook garlic, onion, chopped fennel and pancetta in same dish, stirring, until onion softens. Add paste; cook, stirring, 2 minutes.
5 Meanwhile, rub pork with spice rub.
6 Return pork to dish with wine, undrained tomatoes, stock, the water and rosemary; bring to a boil. Cover; cook in moderate oven 1 hour.
7 Add sliced fennel; cook, covered, in moderate oven 1 hour. Remove pork from dish; discard rind. Cover to keep warm.
8 Meanwhile, cook braising liquid in dish over medium heat, uncovered, until thickened slightly. Return sliced pork to dish; serve pork and sauce with warm italian bread, if desired.

PER SERVING	
total fat	32.8g
saturated fat	10.7g
kilojoules	2525
calories	604
carbohydrates	7.5g
protein	66.5g
fibre	4.6g

SLOW COOKER PORK SUITABLE   PRESSURE COOKER PORK SUITABLE   FREEZE NOT SUITABLE

asian-style braised pork neck

PREPARATION TIME 10 MINUTES **COOKING TIME** 2 HOURS 30 MINUTES **SERVES** 4

1 tablespoon peanut oil

1kg piece pork neck

2 cinnamon sticks

2 star anise

½ cup (125ml) soy sauce

½ cup (125ml) chinese rice wine

¼ cup (55g) firmly packed brown sugar

5cm piece fresh ginger (25g), sliced thinly

4 cloves garlic, quartered

1 medium brown onion (150g), chopped coarsely

1 cup (250ml) water

1 Preheat oven to moderately slow.
2 Heat oil in medium deep flameproof baking dish; cook pork, uncovered, until browned all over. Remove from heat.
3 Add combined spices, soy, wine, sugar, ginger, garlic, onion and the water to pork; turn pork to coat in mixture. Cook, uncovered, in moderately slow oven about 2 hours or until pork is tender, turning every 20 minutes.
4 Remove pork; cover to keep warm. Strain braising liquid through muslin-lined strainer over medium saucepan; bring to a boil. Reduce heat; simmer, uncovered, about 5 minutes or until sauce thickens slighly.
5 Serve pork drizzled with sauce; accompany with steamed gai larn in oyster sauce.

STEAMED GAI LARN IN OYSTER SAUCE
Boil, steam or microwave 1kg gai larn until just tender; drain. Heat 1 tablespoon peanut oil in wok; stir-fry gai larn, 1 tablespoon soy sauce and 2 tablespoons oyster sauce about 2 minutes or until gai larn is tender.

PER SERVING (incl. gai larn)	
total fat	29.6g
saturated fat	8.4g
kilojoules	2592
calories	620
carbohydrates	22.1g
protein	62.1g
fibre	10.4g

SLOW COOKER **SUITABLE UP TO STEP 4**   PRESSURE COOKER **SUITABLE UP TO STEP 4**   FREEZE **SUITABLE**

chicken with rosemary and garlic

PREPARATION TIME 20 MINUTES **COOKING TIME** 55 MINUTES **SERVES** 4

Sugar snap peas, also known as honey snap peas, are fresh plump small peas which are eaten whole, pod and all, similarly to snow peas. They are equally good served raw in salads or, as we suggest here, steamed or microwaved until just tender and eaten as a vegetable accompaniment for a main course.

8 chicken thigh cutlets (1.3kg), skin on

2 tablespoons plain flour

2 teaspoons sweet paprika

1 teaspoon cracked black pepper

1 tablespoon olive oil

4 cloves garlic, unpeeled

2 stalks fresh rosemary

1½ cups (375ml) chicken stock

½ cup (125ml) dry white wine

1 Preheat oven to moderate.
2 Toss chicken in combined flour, paprika and pepper; shake away excess flour mixture from chicken.
3 Heat oil in large flameproof baking dish; cook chicken, in batches, until browned all over.
4 Return chicken to same dish with garlic, rosemary, stock and wine; bring to a boil. Transfer dish to moderate oven; cook, uncovered, about 40 minutes or until chicken is tender and cooked through.
5 Remove chicken from dish; cover to keep warm. Cook pan juices in same dish over medium heat, uncovered, about 5 minutes or until sauce thickens slightly. Divide chicken among serving plates, drizzle with sauce. Serve with steamed sugar snap peas.

PER SERVING	
total fat	40.1g
saturated fat	12.4g
kilojoules	2433
calories	582
carbohydrates	5.5g
protein	43.1g
fibre	1.4g

SLOW COOKER **SUITABLE**   PRESSURE COOKER **SUITABLE UP TO STEP 5**   FREEZE **SUITABLE**

chicken drumettes with roasted capsicum sauce and pilaf

PREPARATION TIME 20 MINUTES **COOKING TIME** 1 HOUR **SERVES** 4

3 large red capsicums (1kg)

1 teaspoon ground cinnamon

½ teaspoon ground cumin

1 teaspoon cracked black pepper

1 tablespoon plain flour

1kg chicken drumettes

¼ cup (60ml) olive oil

1 large brown onion (200g), chopped finely

3 cloves garlic, crushed

1 large tomato (220g), chopped coarsely

1 cup (250ml) chicken stock

1 Quarter capsicums; discard seeds and membranes. Roast under grill or in very hot oven, skin-side up, until skin blisters and blackens. Cover capsicum pieces with plastic wrap or paper for 5 minutes; peel away skin then chop capsicum coarsely.

2 Meanwhile, combine cinnamon, cumin, pepper and flour in large bowl. Add chicken; toss to coat in mixture, shake off excess.

3 Heat 2 tablespoons of the oil in large deep frying pan; cook chicken, in batches, until browned all over.

4 Heat remaining oil in same pan; cook onion and garlic, stirring, until onion softens. Add capsicum, tomato and stock; bring to a boil. Return chicken to pan, reduce heat; simmer, covered, about 30 minutes or until chicken is cooked through.

5 Meanwhile, make pilaf.

6 Remove chicken from pan; blend or process sauce until smooth.

7 Serve chicken on pilaf topped with capsicum sauce; accompany with a salad of baby spinach leaves, if desired.

PILAF Melt 20g butter in medium saucepan; cook 1 clove crushed garlic, stirring, until fragrant. Add 1 cup basmati rice; cook, stirring, 1 minute. Add 1 cup chicken stock and 1 cup water; bring to a boil. Reduce heat; simmer, covered, about 20 minutes or until rice is just tender. Remove from heat; fluff rice with fork. Stir in ¼ cup coarsely chopped fresh flat-leaf parsley and ¼ cup toasted flaked almonds.

PER SERVING (incl. pilaf)	
total fat	28.6g
saturated fat	7.4g
kilojoules	2658
calories	636
carbohydrates	54.5g
protein	40.2g
fibre	5.4g

SLOW COOKER **CHICKEN SUITABLE**   PRESSURE COOKER **CHICKEN SUITABLE**   FREEZE **CHICKEN AND SAUCE SUITABLE**

braised spatchcock with fennel and ouzo

PREPARATION TIME 30 MINUTES **COOKING TIME** 1 HOUR 10 MINUTES **SERVES** 4

Risoni, a tiny rice-shaped pasta similar to orzo, is the perfect accompaniment for this recipe's creamy fennel mixture. While the fennel mixture simmers, cook 500g of risoni in a large saucepan of boiling water. When just tooth-tender (al dente), drain risoni and serve with the spatchcock and fennel.

¼ cup (60ml) olive oil

4 spatchcocks (2kg)

1 medium lemon (140g), quartered

2 large fennel bulbs (1kg), halved, sliced thinly

1 large brown onion (200g), sliced thinly

2 cloves garlic, sliced thinly

¼ cup (60ml) ouzo

2 cups (500ml) chicken stock

3 large zucchini (450g), sliced thinly

2 tablespoons lemon juice

½ cup (125ml) cream

2 tablespoons coarsely chopped fennel fronds

1 Preheat oven to moderately hot.

2 Heat 1 tablespoon of the oil in large deep flameproof baking dish; cook spatchcocks, one at a time, until browned all over. Place one lemon quarter in cavity of each spatchcock.

3 Heat remaining oil in same dish; cook fennel, onion and garlic, stirring, until onion softens. Add ouzo; cook, stirring, until ouzo evaporates. Add stock; bring to a boil. Place spatchcocks on fennel mixture; cook, uncovered, in moderately hot oven about 35 minutes or until spatchcocks are just cooked through.

4 Add zucchini to dish, submerging into fennel mixture; cook, uncovered, in moderately hot oven about 5 minutes or until zucchini is tender. Transfer spatchcocks to large plate; cover to keep warm.

5 Bring fennel mixture to a boil. Add juice and cream; return to a boil. Reduce heat; simmer, uncovered, 5 minutes. Stir in half of the fennel fronds.

6 Using slotted spoon, divide fennel mixture among plates; top with spatchcock. Drizzle with pan juices; sprinkle with remaining fennel fronds, serve with risoni, if desired.

PER SERVING	
total fat	61.4g
saturated fat	20.8g
kilojoules	3407
calories	815
carbohydrates	10g
protein	49.1g
fibre	6.4g

SLOW COOKER SUITABLE UP TO STEP 5   PRESSURE COOKER SUITABLE UP TO STEP 4   FREEZE NOT SUITABLE

braised sweet ginger duck

PREPARATION TIME 20 MINUTES **COOKING TIME** 1 HOUR 50 MINUTES **SERVES** 4

2kg duck

3 cups (750ml) water

½ cup (125ml) chinese cooking wine

⅓ cup (80ml) soy sauce

¼ cup (55g) firmly packed brown sugar

1 whole star anise

3 green onions, halved

3 cloves garlic, quartered

10cm piece fresh ginger (50g), unpeeled, chopped coarsely

2 teaspoons sea salt

1 teaspoon five-spice powder

800g baby bok choy, halved

1 Preheat oven to moderate.

2 Discard neck from duck, wash duck; pat dry with absorbent paper. Score duck in thickest parts of skin; cut duck in half through breastbone and along both sides of backbone, discard backbone. Tuck wings under duck.

3 Place duck, skin-side down, in medium shallow baking dish; add combined water, wine, soy, sugar, star anise, onion, garlic and ginger. Cover; cook in moderate oven about 1 hour or until duck is cooked as desired.

4 Increase oven temperature to hot. Remove duck from braising liquid; strain liquid through muslin-lined sieve into large saucepan. Place duck, skin-side up, on wire rack in same dish. Rub combined salt and five-spice all over duck; roast duck, uncovered, in hot oven about 30 minutes or until skin is crisp.

5 Skim fat from surface of braising liquid; bring to a boil. Reduce heat; simmer, uncovered, 10 minutes. Add bok choy; simmer, covered, about 5 minutes or until bok choy is just tender.

6 Cut duck halves into two pieces; divide bok choy, braising liquid and duck among plates. Serve with steamed jasmine rice, if desired.

Star anise is the dried, star-shaped seed pod of a small evergreen tree grown from Southwest China through Southeast Asia to Japan. Each fruit's pod has, as a rule, eight points having a total span of about 3cm, and each point contains a seed. The star-shaped pod can be used whole as a flavouring or the seeds alone as a spice; both can be used ground.

PER SERVING	
total fat	105.7g
saturated fat	31.7g
kilojoules	4974
calories	1190
carbohydrates	17.9g
protein	40.8g
fibre	3.5g

SLOW COOKER SUITABLE UP TO STEP 4   PRESSURE COOKER SUITABLE UP TO STEP 4   FREEZE NOT SUITABLE

chicken stuffed with ricotta, basil and prosciutto

PREPARATION TIME 30 MINUTES   **COOKING TIME** 2 HOURS **SERVES** 4

Sourdough bread has been around since ancient times and is the "real" French bread, but it became universally known when Isidore Boudin, a French baker in San Francisco, added a local starter (or levain or mother) to his native breadmaking traditions. The name refers not to the taste, which is slightly sweet, but to the bread's singularly natural fermentation process.

8 chicken thigh cutlets (1.3kg)

⅔ cup (130g) ricotta cheese

4 slices prosciutto (60g), halved lengthways

8 large fresh basil leaves

1 tablespoon olive oil

1 medium brown onion (150g), chopped finely

1 medium carrot (120g), chopped finely

1 trimmed celery stalk (100g), chopped finely

2 cloves garlic, chopped finely

2 tablespoons tomato paste

½ cup (125ml) dry white wine

8 small tomatoes (720g), peeled, chopped coarsely

425g can diced tomatoes

½ cup (125ml) water

1 Preheat oven to moderately slow.
2 Using small sharp knife, cut a pocket through thickest part of each cutlet over the bone, push 1 tablespoon of the cheese, one slice of prosciutto and one basil leaf into each pocket; secure pocket closed with toothpick.
3 Heat oil in large deep flameproof baking dish; cook chicken, in batches, until browned all over.
4 Cook onion, carrot, celery and garlic in same dish, stirring, about 5 minutes or until onion softens. Add paste; cook, stirring, 2 minutes. Add wine; bring to a boil. Reduce heat; simmer, uncovered, 1 minute. Add chopped tomato, undrained diced tomatoes and the water; bring to a boil. Reduce heat; simmer, uncovered, 10 minutes.
5 Return chicken to dish, cover; cook in moderately slow oven 1 hour. Uncover; cook in moderately slow oven about 20 minutes or until chicken is cooked through. Remove toothpicks; serve chicken with sourdough, if desired.

PER SERVING	
total fat	46.8g
saturated fat	15.5g
kilojoules	2922
calories	699
carbohydrates	11.2g
protein	53.3g
fibre	5.5g

SLOW COOKER **SUITABLE**   PRESSURE COOKER **SUITABLE**   FREEZE **NOT SUITABLE**

chicken cacciatore with split pea salad

PREPARATION TIME 20 MINUTES (PLUS STANDING TIME) **COOKING TIME** 2 HOURS 10 MINUTES **SERVES** 4

1 cup (200g) green split peas

2 tablespoons olive oil

1.5kg chicken pieces, skin on

1 medium brown onion (150g), chopped finely

½ cup (125ml) dry white wine

2 tablespoons white wine vinegar

½ cup (125ml) chicken stock

410g can crushed tomatoes

¼ cup (70g) tomato paste

½ cup (60g) seeded black olives, chopped coarsely

2 tablespoons drained capers, rinsed, chopped coarsely

2 cloves garlic, crushed

½ cup coarsely chopped fresh flat-leaf parsley

½ cup coarsely chopped fresh basil

1 Place peas in medium bowl, cover with cold water; stand overnight, drain. Rinse under cold water; drain.

2 Heat half of the oil in large deep saucepan; cook chicken, in batches, until browned all over.

3 Cook onion in same pan, stirring, until onion softens. Stir in wine, vinegar, stock, undrained tomatoes and paste.

4 Return chicken to pan, fitting pieces upright and tightly together in single layer; bring to a boil. Reduce heat; simmer, covered, 1 hour. Uncover; simmer about 45 minutes or until chicken is tender. Skim fat from surface; stir in olives.

5 Meanwhile, place peas in large saucepan of boiling water; return to a boil. Reduce heat; simmer, uncovered, about 40 minutes or until peas are tender, drain.

6 Combine peas, capers, garlic, herbs and remaining oil in large bowl. Serve chicken cacciatore with split pea salad.

Capers are a nifty little package of delicious taste with nary a skerrick of fat or carbs! The grey-green buds of a warm climate shrub, capers are sold either dried and salted or pickled in brine. Tiny early-picked baby capers are fuller-flavoured and more expensive than the fully grown version.

PER SERVING	
total fat	37.2g
saturated fat	9.7g
kilojoules	2830
calories	677
carbohydrates	34.1g
protein	47g
fibre	8.5g

SLOW COOKER CHICKEN SUITABLE   PRESSURE COOKER CHICKEN SUITABLE   FREEZE CHICKEN SUITABLE

asian chicken pot au feu

PREPARATION TIME 30 MINUTES **COOKING TIME** 1 HOUR 30 MINUTES **SERVES** 4

Kaffir lime leaves look like two glossy dark-green leaves joined end to end, forming a rounded hourglass shape. They are used, fresh or dried, as a flavouring, like bay leaves or curry leaves, throughout Asia, especially in Thai cooking. Sold fresh, dried or frozen, the dried leaves are less potent so double the number called for in a recipe if you substitute them for fresh leaves.

4 litres (16 cups) water

1.5kg chicken

2 cloves garlic, bruised

2 large carrots (360g), halved, quartered lengthways

10cm stick fresh lemon grass (20g), bruised

2 fresh kaffir lime leaves

2cm piece galangal (10g), sliced thinly

2 fresh long red chillies, halved lengthways

1 teaspoon sichuan peppercorns

½ teaspoon five-spice powder

¼ cup (60ml) mirin

½ cup (125ml) soy sauce

⅓ cup (80ml) kecap manis

350g broccolini, chopped coarsely

1   Bring the water to a boil in large deep saucepan. Add chicken, garlic, carrot, lemon grass, lime leaves, galangal, chilli, peppercorns, five-spice, mirin, sauce and kecap manis; return to a boil. Reduce heat; simmer, uncovered, 1 hour, skimming fat from surface occasionally.

2   Remove chicken; strain broth through muslin-lined sieve into large bowl. Reserve carrot; discard remaining solids. Cover chicken and carrot to keep warm. Return all but 2 cups of the broth to same saucepan; bring to a boil. Cook broccolini in large saucepan of boiling broth, uncovered, until just tender; drain over large bowl. Reserve broth for another use.

3   Meanwhile, place the 2 cups of broth in small saucepan; bring to a boil. Boil rapidly, uncovered, until reduced to 1 cup.

4   Serve chicken with carrot, broccolini, reduced broth and, if desired, steamed jasmine rice.

PER SERVING	
total fat	28.6g
saturated fat	8.8g
kilojoules	2082
calories	498
carbohydrates	16g
protein	41.8g
fibre	6g

SLOW COOKER **CHICKEN SUITABLE**   PRESSURE COOKER **CHICKEN SUITABLE**   FREEZE **CHICKEN SUITABLE**

slow-cooked duck with cabbage and fennel

PREPARATION TIME 20 MINUTES **COOKING TIME** 2 HOURS 20 MINUTES **SERVES** 4

½ small red cabbage (600g), cut into four wedges

1 large leek (500g), chopped coarsely

4 baby fennel bulbs (520g), trimmed, halved lengthways

1 tablespoon fresh rosemary leaves

2 cloves garlic, sliced thinly

1 cup (250ml) chicken stock

⅓ cup (80ml) cider vinegar

2 tablespoons redcurrant jelly

4 duck marylands (1.2kg), trimmed

1 tablespoon salt

1 Preheat oven to moderately slow.
2 Combine cabbage, leek, fennel, rosemary, garlic, stock, vinegar and jelly in medium deep baking dish. Rub duck skin with salt; place duck, skin-side up, on cabbage mixture. Cook, uncovered, in moderately slow oven about 2¼ hours or until duck meat is tender and skin crisp.
3 Meanwhile, make balsamic-roasted potatoes.
4 Strain pan juices through muslin-lined sieve into medium saucepan; cover duck and cabbage mixture to keep warm. Skim fat from surface of pan juices; bring to a boil. Boil, uncovered, about 5 minutes or until sauce thickens slightly.
5 Serve duck, with cabbage mixture and balsamic-roasted potatoes, drizzled with sauce.

BALSAMIC-ROASTED POTATOES Combine 1kg halved small potatoes, 30g melted butter and 2 tablespoons balsamic vinegar in medium baking dish. Roast, uncovered, in moderately slow oven about 1¼ hours or until potatoes are tender and browned lightly, brushing potatoes occasionally with vinegar mixture in dish.

PER SERVING (incl. potatoes)	
total fat	90.4g
saturated fat	29.2g
kilojoules	4719
calories	1129
carbohydrates	39.4g
protein	40.1g
fibre	12.4g

SLOW COOKER **NOT SUITABLE**   PRESSURE COOKER **NOT SUITABLE**   FREEZE **SUITABLE**

lamu chicken

PREPARATION TIME 30 MINUTES **COOKING TIME** 1 HOUR 5 MINUTES **SERVES** 6

20g butter

4 large brown onions (800g), sliced thinly

2 tablespoons white wine vinegar

1 tablespoon brown sugar

2 tablespoons peanut oil

12 chicken drumsticks (1.8kg)

2 cups (400g) basmati rice

2 cinnamon sticks

2 cups (500ml) chicken stock

2 cups (500ml) water

2 limes, cut into wedges

SPICE PASTE

2 ancho chillies

3 cloves garlic, quartered

2cm piece fresh ginger (10g), quartered

1 small green thai chilli, sliced thinly

1 teaspoon cumin seeds

1 teaspoon coriander seeds

1 teaspoon sea salt

1 teaspoon cracked black pepper

½ teaspoon cardamom seeds

4 whole cloves

1 Make spice paste.
2 Melt butter in large deep saucepan; cook onion, stirring, until soft. Add vinegar and sugar; cook, stirring, about 10 minutes or until onion is caramelised. Transfer to medium bowl; cover to keep warm.
3 Heat half of the oil in same pan; cook chicken, in batches, until browned all over.
4 Heat remaining oil in same pan; cook spice paste, stirring, until fragrant. Add rice and half of the caramelised onion; stir to coat in spice mixture.
5 Return chicken to pan with cinnamon, stock and the water; bring to a boil. Reduce heat; simmer, covered tightly, about 30 minutes or until rice is tender and chicken is cooked through. Discard cinnamon sticks.
6 Divide chicken and rice among plates; top with warmed remaining caramelised onion and lime. Serve with a mixed green salad, if desired.

SPICE PASTE Place ancho chillies in small bowl; cover with warm water. Stand 20 minutes; drain. Discard stems and liquid. Using mortar and pestle, crush ancho chillies with remaining ingredients until mixture forms a thick paste.

PER SERVING	
total fat	31.2g
saturated fat	9.7g
kilojoules	2876
calories	688
carbohydrates	60.3g
protein	41.6g
fibre	2.4g

SLOW COOKER **NOT SUITABLE**   PRESSURE COOKER **NOT SUITABLE**   FREEZE **NOT SUITABLE**

creamy chicken korma

PREPARATION TIME 25 MINUTES (PLUS REFRIGERATION TIME) **COOKING TIME** 1 HOUR **SERVES** 4

¼ cup (35g) unsalted cashews

1 teaspoon sesame seeds

500g yogurt

3 cloves garlic, crushed

2cm piece fresh ginger (10g), grated

1 teaspoon dried chilli flakes

½ teaspoon ground turmeric

1kg chicken thigh fillets, diced into 3cm pieces

2 tablespoons vegetable oil

2 medium brown onions (300g), sliced thinly

2 cardamom pods

2 whole cloves

½ teaspoon black cumin seeds

½ cinnamon stick

2 tablespoons lemon juice

⅓ cup (15g) flaked coconut

⅓ cup (50g) unsalted cashews, extra

2 teaspoons kalonji seeds

¼ cup loosely packed fresh coriander leaves

Also known as nigella, kalonji are angular purple-black seeds which are a creamy colour inside and possess a sharp, nutty taste. They are the seeds sprinkled over the top of freshly made pide, Turkish bread, that give it a special sharp, peppery flavour. Kalonji are found in spice shops and Middle-Eastern and Asian food stores.

1 Process nuts and sesame seeds until ground finely. Combine nut mixture with yogurt, garlic, ginger, chilli and turmeric in large bowl; add chicken, toss to coat in marinade. Cover; refrigerate 3 hours or overnight.

2 Heat oil in large saucepan; cook onion, stirring, until soft. Add chicken mixture. Reduce heat; simmer, uncovered, 40 minutes, stirring occasionally.

3 Using mortar and pestle, crush cardamom, cloves and cumin seeds.

4 Add spice mixture, cinnamon and juice to chicken mixture; cook, uncovered, about 10 minutes or until chicken is cooked through.

5 Meanwhile, cook coconut and extra nuts in small frying pan, stirring, until browned lightly. Remove from heat; stir in kalonji seeds.

6 Discard cinnamon from curry; serve curry, sprinkled with coconut mixture, with steamed basmati rice, if desired.

PER SERVING	
total fat	45.7g
saturated fat	13.6g
kilojoules	2918
calories	698
carbohydrates	13.2g
protein	58.1g
fibre	3.7g

SLOW COOKER **CHICKEN SUITABLE**   PRESSURE COOKER **CHICKEN SUITABLE**   FREEZE **NOT SUITABLE**

chicken and merguez cassoulet

PREPARATION TIME 25 MINUTES (PLUS STANDING TIME) **COOKING TIME** 2 HOURS 45 MINUTES **SERVES** 6

Ask your butcher to halve the chicken thigh cutlets for you.

1½ cups (290g) lima beans

1 tablespoon vegetable oil

8 chicken thigh cutlets (1.3kg), halved

6 merguez sausages (480g)

1 large brown onion (200g), chopped coarsely

2 medium carrots (240g), diced into 1cm pieces

2 cloves garlic, chopped finely

4 sprigs fresh thyme

2 tablespoons tomato paste

1 teaspoon finely grated lemon rind

425g can diced tomatoes

1 cup (250ml) chicken stock

1 cup (250ml) water

2 cups (140g) fresh breadcrumbs

GREEN ONION COUSCOUS Place 2 cups chicken stock in medium saucepan; bring to a boil. Remove from heat, stir in 2 cups couscous and 30g butter, cover; stand about 5 minutes or until stock is absorbed, fluffing with fork occasionally. Add 2 thinly sliced green onions; toss gently to combine.

TIP If your grill is too small to brown the entire top of the cassoulet, place it, uncovered, in a moderately hot oven, about 10 minutes or until the breadcrumb crust browns lightly.

1 Place beans in medium bowl, cover with cold water; stand overnight, drain. Rinse under cold water; drain. Cook beans in large saucepan of boiling water, uncovered, 10 minutes; drain.
2 Heat oil in large flameproof casserole dish; cook chicken, in batches, until browned all over. Cook sausages, in batches, in same dish until browned all over. Drain on absorbent paper; halve sausages. Reserve 1 tablespoon of fat from dish; discard remainder.
3 Preheat oven to moderately slow.
4 Heat fat in same dish; cook onion, carrot, garlic and thyme, stirring, until onion softens. Add paste; cook, stirring, 2 minutes. Return chicken to dish with drained beans, rind, undrained tomatoes, stock and the water; bring to a boil. Cover; cook in moderately slow oven 40 minutes.
5 Uncover; cook in moderately slow oven about 1¼ hours or until liquid is almost absorbed and beans are tender.
6 Preheat grill.
7 Sprinkle cassoulet with breadcrumbs; place under preheated grill until breadcrumbs are browned lightly.
8 Meanwhile, make green onion coucous.
9 Serve cassoulet with green onion couscous.

PER SERVING (incl. couscous)	
total fat	53.1g
saturated fat	20.8g
kilojoules	4623
calories	1106
carbohydrates	93.9g
protein	61.6g
fibre	14.9g

SLOW COOKER **CHICKEN SUITABLE UP TO STEP 6**   PRESSURE COOKER **CHICKEN SUITABLE UP TO STEP 4**   FREEZE **SUITABLE**

quail au vin

PREPARATION TIME 20 MINUTES **COOKING TIME** 1 HOUR 20 MINUTES **SERVES** 4

8 quails (1.6kg)

6 slices pancetta (90g), chopped coarsely

2 tablespoons olive oil

8 shallots (200g)

3 cups (750ml) dry red wine

1 cup (250ml) chicken stock

1 tablespoon tomato paste

2 cloves garlic, crushed

1 bay leaf

3 sprigs fresh thyme

2 tablespoons plain flour

20g butter

100g button mushrooms

100g swiss brown mushrooms, halved

100g fresh shiitake mushrooms

⅓ cup coarsely chopped fresh flat-leaf parsley

There are a vast number of different mushrooms freely available to us today. Here we used button, a small, white cultivated mushroom; swiss brown (also known as cremini or roman), a robust, full-bodied fungi; and shiitake, a mushroom with a rich, "wild" flavour and dense texture.

1 Rinse quails under cold water; pat dry with absorbent paper. Discard necks and wings from quails.
2 Meanwhile, cook pancetta in large deep saucepan until crisp; remove from pan. Heat oil in same dish; cook quails, in batches, until browned all over.
3 Return pancetta and quails to dish with shallots, wine, stock, paste, garlic, bay leaf and thyme; bring to a boil. Reduce heat; simmer, covered, 45 minutes.
4 Place flour in small bowl; using fork, gradually blend flour with 1 cup of the braising liquid. Add to quail mixture; stir until mixture boils and thickens slightly.
5 Meanwhile, heat butter in large frying pan; cook mushrooms, stirring, until browned lightly.
6 Stir mushrooms and half of the parsley into quail mixture. Sprinkle quail au vin with remaining parsley; serve accompanied with tagliatelle or fettuccine, if desired.

PER SERVING	
total fat	41.7g
saturated fat	11.9g
kilojoules	3102
calories	742
carbohydrates	10.4g
protein	51g
fibre	3.1g

SLOW COOKER QUAIL SUITABLE   PRESSURE COOKER QUAIL SUITABLE UP TO STEP 4   FREEZE NOT SUITABLE

smoky octopus stew with red wine and olives

PREPARATION TIME 20 MINUTES **COOKING TIME** 1 HOUR 10 MINUTES **SERVES** 4

Spain grows the particular large round pepper called pimenton that is smoked before being ground. It is sold as three individual paprikas — dulce (sweet), agridulce (bittersweet) and picante (spicy hot). The sweeter or more delicately flavoured paprikas are used mainly for colouring and just a hint of flavour while the heat of a spicy paprika is for the cook who likes this seasoning to dominate the dish in which it's used.

1kg cleaned baby octopus

2 bay leaves

2 tablespoons olive oil

2 cloves garlic, crushed

1 large brown onion (200g), sliced thinly

1½ teaspoons bittersweet smoked paprika

5 medium tomatoes (750g), peeled, chopped coarsely

2 tablespoons tomato paste

¾ cup (180ml) dry red wine

⅓ cup (50g) drained sun-dried tomatoes, chopped coarsely

¼ cup (60ml) water

1¼ cups (200g) seeded kalamata olives

2 tablespoons coarsely chopped fresh flat-leaf parsley

1 Cut heads from octopus; cut tentacles into two pieces.
2 Place octopus and bay leaves in large saucepan of water; bring to a boil. Reduce heat; simmer, covered, about 30 minutes or until octopus is just tender, drain. Discard bay leaves.
3 Heat oil in same cleaned pan; cook garlic and onion, stirring, until onions softens. Add paprika, fresh tomato, tomato paste, wine, sun-dried tomato, the water and octopus; bring to a boil. Reduce heat; simmer, covered, 30 minutes. Stir in olives.
4 Sprinkle stew with parsley; serve with a loaf of warmed sourdough bread, if desired.

PER SERVING	
total fat	15.1g
saturated fat	2.4g
kilojoules	2169
calories	519
carbohydrates	23.8g
protein	63.6g
fibre	5.7g

SLOW COOKER **NOT SUITABLE**   PRESSURE COOKER **NOT SUITABLE**   FREEZE **NOT SUITABLE**

stuffed squid saganaki

PREPARATION TIME 50 MINUTES **COOKING TIME** 45 MINUTES **SERVES** 4

8 small whole squid (600g)

¼ cup (40g) seeded kalamata olives, chopped coarsely

1 teaspoon finely grated lemon rind

¼ teaspoon dried chilli flakes

200g fetta cheese, crumbled

2 teaspoons fresh thyme leaves

1 tablespoon olive oil

1 small red onion (100g), chopped finely

1 clove garlic, crushed

½ cup (125ml) dry white wine

1 cinnamon stick

2 x 400g cans diced tomatoes

3 sprigs fresh thyme

2 teaspoons white sugar

1 Gently separate bodies and tentacles of squid by pulling on tentacles. Cut head from tentacles just below eyes; discard head. Trim long tentacle of each squid; remove the clear quill from inside body. Peel inside flaps from bodies with salted fingers, then peel away dark skin. Wash squid well and pat dry with absorbent paper.

2 Combine olives, rind, chilli, three-quarters of the cheese and half of the thyme leaves in small bowl; stuff cheese mixture into squid bodies. Place tentacles inside opening; secure tentacles to squid with toothpicks. Cover; refrigerate until required.

3 Heat oil in large deep frying pan; cook onion and garlic, stirring, until onion softens. Add wine; bring to a boil. Reduce heat; simmer, uncovered, until liquid is reduced by half.

4 Add cinnamon, undrained tomatoes, thyme sprigs and sugar; bring to a boil. Reduce heat; simmer, uncovered, about 10 minutes or until sauce thickens slightly. Add stuffed squid to pan; simmer, covered, about 15 minutes or until squid are cooked through, turning once halfway through cooking time. Add remaining cheese and remaining thyme leaves; stir until cheese melts slightly. Remove toothpicks; serve with greek-style bread, if desired.

Saganaki, despite sounding vaguely Japanese, is the traditional Greek name for a snack or entrée of floured, herbed then fried cheese (fetta, kasseri, haloumi or kefalograviera), which is sprinkled with lemon juice and eaten with bread. It has evolved, however, into a descriptive culinary term for any dish that uses cooked cheese as a main ingredient, such as the saganaki prawns found on many restaurant menus.

PER SERVING	
total fat	18.6g
saturated fat	8.9g
kilojoules	1580
calories	378
carbohydrates	11.7g
protein	36.1g
fibre	3g

SLOW COOKER **NOT SUITABLE** PRESSURE COOKER **NOT SUITABLE** FREEZE **NOT SUITABLE**

seafood stew with chermoulla

PREPARATION TIME 30 MINUTES **COOKING TIME** 30 MINUTES **SERVES** 4

Chermoulla is a Moroccan blend of fresh herbs, spices and condiments traditionally used for preserving or seasoning meat and fish. We used our chermoulla blend here as a quick flavouring for the stew, but you can also use it as a sauce or marinade. You can keep freshly made chermoulla in the refrigerator, covered with a thin layer of olive oil to preserve it, for up to a month.

500g black mussels

800g uncooked medium king prawns

300g kingfish fillet, skinned

1 squid hood (150g)

1 tablespoon olive oil

1 large brown onion (200g), chopped finely

3 cloves garlic, crushed

1 medium red capsicum (200g), chopped finely

½ cup (125ml) dry white wine

1 cup (250ml) fish stock

400g can diced tomatoes

CHERMOULLA

½ cup finely chopped fresh coriander

½ cup finely chopped fresh flat-leaf parsley

1 clove garlic, crushed

2 tablespoons white wine vinegar

2 tablespoons lemon juice

½ teaspoon ground cumin

2 tablespoons olive oil

1 Scrub mussels; remove beards. Shell and devein prawns, leaving tails intact. Dice fish into 3cm pieces. Cut squid down centre to open out; score inside in diagonal pattern then cut into thick strips.
2 Heat oil in large saucepan; cook onion, garlic and capsicum, stirring, until onion softens. Stir in wine; cook, uncovered, until wine is almost evaporated. Add stock and undrained tomatoes; bring to a boil. Add seafood, reduce heat; simmer, covered, about 5 minutes or until squid is tender and mussels open (discard any that do not).
3 Meanwhile, combine ingredients for chermoulla in small bowl.
4 Stir half of the chermoulla into stew. Divide stew among bowls; divide remaining chermoulla over the top of each bowl. Serve with a warmed baguette, if desired.

PER SERVING	
total fat	17.5g
saturated fat	3g
kilojoules	1714
calories	410
carbohydrates	8.7g
protein	48.6g
fibre	3.5g

SLOW COOKER **NOT SUITABLE**   PRESSURE COOKER **NOT SUITABLE**   FREEZE **NOT SUITABLE**

kingfish and tomato tagine

PREPARATION TIME 20 MINUTES COOKING TIME 40 MINUTES SERVES 4

2 tablespoons olive oil

2 large brown onions (400g), chopped coarsely

6 cloves garlic, chopped finely

1 fresh small red thai chilli, chopped finely

4 anchovy fillets, drained, chopped finely

¾ cup coarsely chopped fresh flat-leaf parsley

1 cup coarsely chopped fresh coriander

¾ cup coarsely chopped fresh mint

200g mushrooms, quartered

2 trimmed celery stalks (200g), sliced thickly

2 teaspoons ground cumin

2 x 425g cans diced tomatoes

4 kingfish cutlets (1kg)

1 medium lemon (140g), cut into wedges

2 tablespoons fresh flat-leaf parsley leaves

1 Preheat oven to moderately hot.
2 Heat oil in large deep flameproof baking dish; cook onion, garlic and chilli, stirring, until onion softens. Add anchovy, chopped herbs, mushrooms, celery and cumin; cook, stirring, 5 minutes.
3 Add undrained tomatoes; bring to a boil. Add fish, submerging it in the tomato mixture; return to a boil. Cook, uncovered, in moderately hot oven about 20 minutes or until liquid has almost evaporated and fish is cooked as desired.
4 Meanwhile, make tomato and herb salad. Divide fish and lemon wedge among serving plates; sprinkle with parsley. Serve with salad and, if desired, steamed long-grain white rice.

TOMATO AND HERB SALAD Place 5 coarsely chopped medium tomatoes, 2 tablespoons chopped fresh mint, ¼ cup chopped fresh flat-leaf parsley and 2 tablespoons chopped fresh dill in medium bowl. Place 2 cloves crushed garlic, 2 tablespoons lemon juice, 1 tablespoon olive oil and 2 teaspoons white vinegar in screw-top jar; shake well. Drizzle dressing over salad; toss to combine.

PER SERVING (incl. salad)	
total fat	20.9g
saturated fat	4g
kilojoules	2161
calories	517
carbohydrates	18.9g
protein	61.3g
fibre	12.9g

SLOW COOKER **NOT SUITABLE**   PRESSURE COOKER **NOT SUITABLE**   FREEZE **SUITABLE**

anchovy and garlic tuna with tomato and oregano

PREPARATION TIME 20 MINUTES **COOKING TIME** 25 MINUTES SERVES 4

FETTA AND BLACK OLIVE MASH Boil, steam or microwave 1kg coarsely chopped potato until tender; drain. Mash potato in large bowl with 1 tablespoon olive oil until smooth. Stir in ⅔ cup warmed buttermilk, 200g finely chopped fetta and ½ cup thinly sliced black olives. Drizzle with another tablespoon of olive oil.

1kg tuna fillet, trimmed, skinned

3 cloves garlic, sliced thinly

¼ cup firmly packed fresh oregano leaves

8 drained anchovy fillets, halved

¼ cup (60ml) olive oil

1 large brown onion (200g), sliced thinly

4 large egg tomatoes (360g), seeded, chopped coarsely

¼ cup (60ml) balsamic vinegar

2 tablespoons dry white wine

¼ cup (60ml) fish stock

1 tablespoon drained baby capers, rinsed

¼ cup coarsely chopped fresh basil

1 Preheat oven to moderately hot.
2 Using sharp knife, make 16 cuts in tuna; press 16 slices of the garlic, 16 oregano leaves and anchovy halves into cuts.
3 Heat 2 tablespoons of the oil in medium deep flameproof baking dish; cook tuna, uncovered, until browned. Remove from dish.
4 Heat remaining oil in same dish; cook onion, stirring, until soft. Combine tomato, vinegar, wine, stock, remaining garlic and remaining oregano in dish then add tuna; bring to a boil. Cook, uncovered, in moderately hot oven about 10 minutes or until tuna is cooked as desired. Remove tuna from dish; slice thinly. Stir capers and basil into sauce in dish.
5 Meanwhile, make fetta and black olive mash. Serve tuna with sauce and mash.

PER SERVING (incl. mash)	
total fat	50.8g
saturated fat	17.4g
kilojoules	4021
calories	962
carbohydrates	41.5g
protein	82g
fibre	5.9g

SLOW COOKER **NOT SUITABLE**   PRESSURE COOKER **NOT SUITABLE**   FREEZE **NOT** SUITABLE

japanese seafood hotpot

PREPARATION TIME 20 MINUTES (PLUS REFRIGERATION TIME) **COOKING TIME** 20 MINUTES **SERVES** 4

*We used monkfish in this recipe, but you can use any firm white
fish such as perch or blue-eye fillets.*

12 medium black mussels (300g)

12 uncooked medium king prawns (540g)

2 teaspoons cooking sake

1 tablespoon japanese soy sauce

2 teaspoons mirin

12 scallops without roe (300g)

400g firm white fish fillets, diced into 4cm pieces

1 tablespoon vegetable oil

2 cloves garlic, crushed

5cm piece fresh ginger (25g), chopped finely

3 cups (750ml) fish stock

1 cup (250ml) water

¼ cup (60ml) cooking sake, extra

¼ cup (60ml) japanese soy sauce, extra

1 teaspoon powdered dashi

1 small kumara (250g), halved lengthways, sliced thinly

250g spinach, chopped coarsely

2 green onions, chopped coarsely

270g dried udon

1 Scrub mussels; remove beards. Shell and devein prawns, leaving
   tails intact.
2 Combine sake, soy and mirin in large bowl; add mussels, prawns,
   scallops and fish, toss seafood to coat in mixture.
3 Heat oil in large saucepan; cook garlic and ginger, stirring, until
   fragrant. Add stock, the water, extra sake, extra soy and dashi;
   bring to a boil. Add kumara; cook, uncovered, 2 minutes. Add
   undrained seafood; cook, covered, about 5 minutes or until mussels
   open (discard any that do not). Add spinach and onion; cook,
   uncovered, until spinach just wilts.
4 Meanwhile, cook udon in large saucepan of boiling water, uncovered,
   until just tender; drain.
5 Divide udon among bowls; top with seafood mixture.

Dashi is the basic stock
used in nearly every
Japanese dish, from
a spoonful or two in
dipping sauces to far
greater amounts in the
broths of one-pan dishes
such as shabu-shabu,
sukiyaki or casserole-
like hotpots such as the
one we've made here.
Available in concentrated
liquid as well as granule
or powdered form, the
amount of dashi used can
be adjusted to suit your
personal taste.

PER SERVING	
total fat	7.8g
saturated fat	1.3g
kilojoules	2307
calories	552
carbohydrates	57.3g
protein	56.8g
fibre	4.5g

SLOW COOKER **NOT SUITABLE**   PRESSURE COOKER **NOT SUITABLE**   FREEZE **SUITABLE**

four-cheese pasta bake

PREPARATION TIME 20 MINUTES COOKING TIME 30 MINUTES SERVES 6

500g penne

4 green onions, chopped finely

½ cup (75g) drained semi-dried tomatoes, chopped coarsely

2 tablespoons olive oil

2 cloves garlic, crushed

¼ cup coarsely chopped fresh basil

½ loaf turkish bread (220g), diced into 1cm pieces

FOUR-CHEESE SAUCE

50g butter

⅓ cup (50g) plain flour

1 litre (4 cups) milk

⅓ cup (35g) finely grated fontina cheese

¾ cup (75g) finely grated mozzarella cheese

¾ cup (60g) finely grated parmesan cheese

100g gorgonzola cheese, crumbled

PARMESAN AND BABY SPINACH SALAD Place 100g baby spinach leaves, 50g shaved parmesan cheese and 1 tablespoon toasted pine nuts in large bowl. Combine 2 tablespoons balsamic vinegar and 1 tablespoon olive oil in screw-top jar; shake well. Drizzle dressing over salad; toss gently to combine.

1 Preheat oven to moderate. Lightly grease deep 3-litre (12-cup) baking dish.
2 Cook pasta in large saucepan of boiling water until just tender.
3 Meanwhile, make four-cheese sauce.
4 Drain pasta; return to same pan with onion, tomato and cheese sauce; toss gently to combine. Transfer pasta mixture to prepared baking dish.
5 Combine oil, garlic and basil in medium bowl; add bread, toss gently to combine topping mixture.
6 Sprinkle topping mixture over pasta bake in even layer; cook, uncovered, in moderate oven about 15 minutes or until topping is browned lightly and pasta bake is cooked through.
7 Meanwhile, make parmesan and baby spinach salad. Serve pasta bake with spinach salad.

FOUR-CHEESE SAUCE Melt butter in medium saucepan, add flour; cook, stirring, until mixture bubbles and thickens. Gradually add milk; cook, stirring, until sauce boils and thickens. Remove from heat, add cheeses; stir until smooth.

PER SERVING (incl. salad)	
total fat	38.9g
saturated fat	17.5g
kilojoules	3724
calories	891
carbohydrates	88.2g
protein	36.4g
fibre	7.2g

SLOW COOKER NOT SUITABLE   PRESSURE COOKER NOT SUITABLE   FREEZE NOT SUITABLE

chickpea vegetable braise with cumin couscous

PREPARATION TIME 20 MINUTES (PLUS STANDING TIME) **COOKING TIME** 1 HOUR 25 MINUTES **SERVES** 4

1 cup (200g) dried chickpeas

2 tablespoons olive oil

2 small leeks (400g), chopped coarsely

2 medium carrots (240g), cut into batons

2 cloves garlic, crushed

1 tablespoon finely chopped fresh rosemary

2 tablespoons white wine vinegar

2 cups (500ml) vegetable stock

100g baby spinach leaves

¼ cup (60ml) lemon juice

2 tablespoons olive oil, extra

2 cloves garlic, crushed, extra

CUMIN COUSCOUS

1 cup (250ml) boiling water

1 cup (200g) couscous

1 tablespoon olive oil

1 teaspoon ground cumin

TOMATO AND RED ONION SALAD
Arrange 4 thinly sliced medium tomatoes and 2 thinly sliced medium red onions on serving platter; drizzle with 2 tablespoons red wine vinegar and 1 tablespoon olive oil. Sprinkle with cracked black pepper.

1 Place chickpeas in medium bowl, cover with cold water; stand overnight, drain. Rinse under cold water; drain. Place chickpeas in medium saucepan of boiling water. Return to a boil, reduce heat; simmer, uncovered, about 40 minutes or until chickpeas are tender. Drain.

2 Meanwhile, preheat oven to moderately slow.

3 Heat oil in large deep flameproof baking dish; cook leek and carrot, stirring, until just tender. Add garlic, rosemary and chickpeas; cook, stirring, until fragrant. Add vinegar and stock; bring to a boil. Cover; cook in moderately slow oven 30 minutes.

4 Meanwhile, make the cumin couscous. Make the tomato and red onion salad.

5 Remove dish from oven; stir in spinach, juice, extra oil and extra garlic. Serve chickpea vegetable braise with couscous and tomato and red onion salad.

CUMIN COUSCOUS Combine the water and couscous in medium heatproof bowl, cover; stand about 5 minutes or until liquid is absorbed, fluffing with fork occasionally. Add oil and cumin; toss gently to combine.

PER SERVING (incl. salad)	
total fat	31.6g
saturated fat	4.6g
kilojoules	2717
calories	650
carbohydrates	68.7g
protein	21.3g
fibre	13.8g

SLOW COOKER NOT SUITABLE   PRESSURE COOKER CHICKPEAS SUITABLE   FREEZE NOT SUITABLE

banana chillies with potato and green olive stuffing

PREPARATION TIME 50 MINUTES **COOKING TIME** 1 HOUR 10 MINUTES **SERVES** 4

This recipe is our version of the classic Mexican "chiles rellenos", stuffed Anaheim peppers. We used banana chillies, also known as wax chillies, Hungarian peppers or sweet banana peppers, which are almost as mild as capsicum but also possess a slightly sweet sharp taste.
Sold in varying degrees of ripeness, they are available in pale olive green, yellow and red.

40g butter

2 tablespoons olive oil

3 cloves garlic, crushed

2 teaspoons ground cumin

2 teaspoons dried oregano

600g potatoes, diced into 1cm pieces

3 large tomatoes (660g), diced into 1cm pieces

1 cup (120g) seeded green olives, chopped coarsely

2 cups (240g) coarsely grated cheddar cheese

8 red or yellow banana chillies (1.3kg)

TOMATO SAUCE

1 tablespoon olive oil

1 clove garlic, crushed

1 medium red onion (170g), chopped coarsely

1 tablespoon ground cumin

2 teaspoons dried oregano

2 x 425g cans diced tomatoes

½ cup (125ml) water

1 Preheat oven to moderate.
2 Heat butter and oil in large frying pan; cook garlic, cumin, oregano and potato, stirring occasionally, about 10 minutes or until potato browns lightly. Add tomato and olives; cook, stirring, about 10 minutes or until liquid has evaporated. Transfer to large bowl; stir in cheese.
3 Meanwhile, using sharp knife, make a small horizontal cut in a chilli 1cm below stem, then make lengthways slit in chilli, starting from horizontal cut and ending 1cm from tip, taking care not to cut all the way through chilli; discard membrane and seeds. Repeat process with remaining chillies. Carefully divide filling among chillies, securing each closed with a toothpick.
4 Make tomato sauce. Place chillies on tomato sauce in dish, cover; cook in moderate oven about 40 minutes or until chillies are tender. Serve chillies with tomato sauce and a mixed green salad, if desired.

TOMATO SAUCE Heat oil in large deep flameproof baking dish; cook garlic, onion, cumin and oregano, stirring, until onion softens. Add undrained tomatoes and the water; bring to a boil. Reduce heat; simmer, uncovered, 10 minutes.

PER SERVING	
total fat	43.8g
saturated fat	20.3g
kilojoules	2725
calories	652
carbohydrates	39.9g
protein	24.4g
fibre	11.2g

SLOW COOKER NOT SUITABLE   PRESSURE COOKER NOT SUITABLE   FREEZE NOT SUITABLE

roasted root vegetable ratatouille

PREPARATION TIME 40 MINUTES **COOKING TIME** 1 HOUR 30 MINUTES **SERVES** 6

800g celeriac, trimmed, chopped coarsely

2 large carrots (360g), chopped coarsely

2 medium parsnips (500g), chopped coarsely

2 medium kumara (800g), chopped coarsely

⅓ cup (80ml) olive oil

1 large brown onion (200g), chopped finely

3 cloves garlic, crushed

¼ cup loosely packed fresh oregano leaves

1 tablespoon tomato paste

2 x 425g cans crushed tomatoes

½ cup (125ml) dry red wine

1 cup (250ml) water

½ cup (40g) coarsely grated parmesan cheese

2½ cups (250g) coarsely grated mozzarella cheese

1 cup (70g) fresh breadcrumbs

2 teaspoons finely grated lemon rind

½ cup coarsely chopped fresh flat-leaf parsley

2 tablespoons coarsely chopped fresh oregano

Celeriac, a member of the celery family, is a tuberous brown-skinned root having a white flesh that tastes like a very earthy, more pungent celery. Sometimes called knob celery, celeriac is the cooking celery of Northern Europe. Peeled and diced, it can be used raw in salads or on a crudités platter; steamed or boiled, it can be mashed like potato or diced and served as a cooked vegetable.

1 Combine celeriac, carrot, parsnip, kumara and half of the oil in large deep baking dish. Roast, uncovered, in hot oven about 50 minutes or until vegetables are tender and browned lightly, stirring halfway through cooking time.

2 Meanwhile, heat remaining oil in large saucepan; cook onion, garlic and oregano leaves, stirring, until onion softens. Add paste; cook, stirring, 1 minute. Add undrained tomatoes, wine and the water; bring to a boil. Boil, uncovered, 10 minutes.

3 Preheat oven to hot.

4 Add tomato mixture to vegetables in dish; toss gently to combine. Sprinkle with combined cheeses, breadcrumbs, rind, parsley and chopped oregano. Cook, uncovered, in hot oven about 20 minutes or until top browns lightly. Serve with a lemon vinaigrette-dressed green leafy salad, if desired.

PER SERVING	
total fat	24.7g
saturated fat	9.1g
kilojoules	2090
calories	500
carbohydrates	43.9g
protein	22.1g
fibre	12.7g

SLOW COOKER NOT SUITABLE   PRESSURE COOKER NOT SUITABLE   FREEZE NOT SUITABLE

potato and kumara curry

PREPARATION TIME 20 MINUTES **COOKING TIME** 1 HOUR 25 MINUTES **SERVES** 4

In Indian cooking terms, masala simply means ground or blended spices (incidentally, the word has become slang for "mix" or "mixture"), so a masala can be whole spices, or a paste or a powder. Garam masala, used here, is a North Indian blend of spices based on varying proportions of cardamom, cinnamon, coriander, cloves, fennel and cumin, roasted and ground together.

2 tablespoons vegetable oil

1 teaspoon fenugreek seeds

1 teaspoon ground cumin

1 teaspoon ground coriander

1 teaspoon garam masala

½ teaspoon ground turmeric

2 cloves garlic, crushed

1 long green chilli, sliced thinly

700g potatoes, chopped coarsely

1 large kumara (500g), chopped coarsely

2 x 400g can crushed tomatoes

1 cup (250ml) vegetable stock

¼ cup (70g) yogurt

2 large brown onions (400g), sliced thinly

½ cup loosely packed fresh coriander leaves

1 Heat half of the oil in large saucepan; cook spices, garlic and chilli, stirring, until fragrant. Add potato and kumara; cook, stirring, 5 minutes.

2 Stir in undrained tomatoes and stock; bring to a boil. Reduce heat; simmer, covered, about 1 hour or until potato and kumara are tender. Stir in yogurt.

3 Meanwhile, heat remaining oil in medium frying pan; cook onion, stirring, until onion browns lightly.

4 Divide curry among serving plates; top with onion and coriander. Serve with steamed basmati rice, if desired.

PER SERVING	
total fat	10.8g
saturated fat	1.7g
kilojoules	1342
calories	321
carbohydrates	45g
protein	10.1g
fibre	8.4g

SLOW COOKER CURRY SUITABLE   PRESSURE COOKER CURRY SUITABLE   FREEZE SUITABLE

potato and cheese kofta with tomato tamarind sauce

PREPARATION TIME 30 MINUTES (PLUS STANDING TIME) **COOKING TIME** 35 MINUTES **SERVES** 4

2 medium potatoes (400g)

2 tablespoons finely chopped fresh coriander

½ cup (75g) toasted unsalted cashews, chopped finely

½ cup (60g) frozen peas, thawed

vegetable oil, for deep-frying

4 hard-boiled eggs, halved

CHEESE

1 litre (4 cups) milk

2 tablespoons lemon juice

TOMATO TAMARIND SAUCE

1 tablespoon olive oil

1 clove garlic, crushed

3cm piece fresh ginger (15g), grated

½ teaspoon dried chilli flakes

1 teaspoon ground cumin

1 teaspoon ground coriander

½ teaspoon mustard seeds

¼ cup (60ml) tamarind concentrate

2 x 400g cans crushed tomatoes

Tamarind is associated with the food of India and South-East Asia, but is actually the product of a native tropical African tree that grows as high as 25 metres. The tree produces clusters of brown "hairy" pods, each of which is filled with seeds and a viscous pulp that are dried and pressed into the blocks of tamarind found in Asian supermarkets.

1 Make cheese. Make tomato tamarind sauce.

2 Meanwhile, boil, steam or microwave potato until tender; drain.

3 Mash potato in large bowl; stir in cheese, coriander, nuts and peas. Heat oil in wok; deep-fry level tablespoons of the potato mixture, in batches, until cooked through. Drain on absorbent paper.

4 Add koftas to tomato tamarind sauce; simmer, uncovered, 5 minutes. Divide koftas and sauce among serving plates; top with egg.

CHEESE Bring milk to a boil in medium saucepan. Remove from heat; stir in juice. Cool 10 minutes. Pour through muslin-lined sieve into medium bowl; stand cheese mixture in sieve over bowl for 40 minutes. Discard liquid in bowl.

TOMATO TAMARIND SAUCE Heat oil in large saucepan; cook garlic and ginger, stirring, until fragrant. Add chilli, spices and seeds; cook, stirring, 1 minute. Add tamarind and undrained tomatoes; bring to a boil. Reduce heat; simmer, uncovered, 5 minutes.

PER SERVING	
total fat	29.7g
saturated fat	6.7g
kilojoules	2144
calories	513
carbohydrates	37g
protein	25.3g
fibre	6.2g

SLOW COOKER **NOT** SUITABLE   PRESSURE COOKER **NOT** SUITABLE   FREEZE **NOT** SUITABLE

glossary

ALLSPICE also known as pimento or jamaican pepper; so-named because it tastes like a combination of nutmeg, cumin, clove and cinnamon — all spices.

ALMONDS flat, pointy ended nuts with pitted brown shell enclosing a creamy white kernel that is covered by a brown skin.
flaked paper-thin slices.
slivered cut lengthways.

ANISE also known as aniseed or sweet cumin; has a strong licorice flavour. Available whole or ground.

BACON RASHERS also known as slices of bacon.

BARLEY a nutritious grain used in soups and stews. Hulled barley is the least processed form of barley and is high in fibre. Pearl barley has had the husk discarded and been hulled and polished, much the same as rice.

BEANS
black-eyed also known as black-eyed peas.
borlotti also known as roman beans; can be sold fresh or dried.
kidney medium-sized red bean, slightly floury, yet sweet in flavour; sold dried or canned.
lima large, beige, flat, kidney-shaped bean. Can be dried or canned. Also known as butter beans.

BOK CHOY also known as bak choy, pak choi, chinese white cabbage or chinese chard. Has a fresh, mild mustard taste; use both stems and leaves. **Baby bok choy** is smaller and more tender than bok choy.

BREADCRUMBS
packaged fine-textured, crunchy, purchased, white breadcrumbs.
stale one- or two-day-old bread made into crumbs by blending or processing.

BROCCOLINI a cross between broccoli and chinese kale. Is milder and sweeter than broccoli.

BUTTER use salted or unsalted (sweet) butter; 125g is equal to 1 stick butter.

CAPERS the grey-green buds of a warm climate (usually Mediterranean) shrub, sold either dried and salted or pickled in a vinegar brine; tiny young ones, called baby capers, are also available.

CAPSICUM also known as bell pepper or, simply, pepper. Discard seeds and membranes before use.

CARDAMOM one of the world's most expensive spices; has a distinctive aromatic, sweetly rich flavour. Purchase in pod, seed or ground form.

CAYENNE PEPPER a long, thin-fleshed, extremely hot, dried red chilli, usually purchased ground.

CELERIAC tuberous root with brown skin, white flesh and celery-like flavour.

CHEESE
fontina a smooth firm cheese with a nutty taste and a brown or red rind.
gorgonzola a creamy Italian blue cheese having a mild, sweet taste.
mozzarella soft, spun-curd cheese; originated in southern Italy where it is traditionally made from water buffalo milk.

CHICKPEAS also called garbanzos, hummus or channa; an irregularly round, sandy-coloured legume used extensively in Mediterranean and Latin cooking.

CHILLI use rubber gloves when seeding and chopping fresh chillies as they can burn your skin. Removing seeds and membranes lessens the heat level.

chipotle a dried, smoked jalapeño chilli. It has a deep, intensely smokey flavour, rather than a searing heat. They are dark brown in appearance. Available in cans.
flakes crushed, dried chillies.
green these are generally unripened thai chillies, but sometimes varieties that are ripe when green, such as habanero, poblano or serrano chillies are used.
thai red small, bright red with a medium heat.

CHINESE COOKING WINE made from rice, wheat, sugar and salt, with 13.5% alcohol; available from Asian food stores. Mirin or sherry can be substituted.

CHORIZO a sausage of Spanish origin, made of coarsely ground pork and highly seasoned with garlic and chillies.

CIABATTA in Italian, the word means slipper, which is the traditional shape of this popular crisp-crusted white bread.

CLOVES dried flower buds of a tropical tree; can be used whole or ground. Have a strong scent and taste, so use them minimally.

COCONUT
flaked dried flaked coconut flesh.
milk the second pressing (less rich) from grated mature coconut flesh.

COUSCOUS made from semolina; a fine, grain-like cereal product, originally from North Africa.

CUMIN also known as zeera, available in ground or seed form.

DASHI basic fish and seaweed stock made from dried bonito (a type of fish) flakes and kelp (kombu). Available from Asian specialty stores.

EGGPLANT also known as aubergine.

FENNEL also known as finocchio or anise.

FENUGREEK hard, dried seed usually sold ground.

FIVE-SPICE POWDER a fragrant mixture of star anise, ground cinnamon, cloves, sichuan pepper and fennel seeds.

FLOUR
plain an all-purpose flour, made from wheat.
self-raising plain flour sifted with baking powder in the proportion of 1 cup flour to 2 teaspoons baking powder.

GAI LARN also known as kanah, gai lum, chinese broccoli and chinese kale; appreciated more for its stems than its coarse leaves. Can be steamed and stir-fried.

GALANGAL also known as ka, a rhizome with a hot ginger-citrusy flavour; used similarly to ginger and garlic. Fresh ginger can be substituted, but the flavour of the dish will not be the same.

GARAM MASALA a blend of cardamom, cinnamon, cloves, coriander, fennel and cumin.

GINGER also known as green or root ginger.
ground also known as powdered ginger; cannot be substituted for fresh ginger.

GREEN SPLIT PEAS also known as field peas; used in soups and stews.

HERBS when specified, we used dried (not ground) herbs in the proportion of 1:4 for fresh herbs (1 teaspoon dried herbs equals 4 teaspoons chopped fresh herbs).
bay leaves aromatic leaves from the bay tree used to flavour soups, stocks and casseroles.

coriander also known as pak chee, cilantro or chinese parsley; bright-green-leafed herb with a pungent flavour. Stems and roots may be used; wash well before chopping.

marjoram sweet and mild tasting, used to season meats and fish.

parsley, flat-leaf also known as continental or italian parsley.

KAFFIR LIME LEAVES looks like two glossy dark green leaves joined end to end, forming a rounded hourglass shape. Sold fresh, dried or frozen. A strip of fresh lime peel can be substituted for each kaffir lime leaf.

KALONJI also known as nigella or black onion seeds; are angular seeds, black on the outside and creamy within, having a sharp nutty flavour.

kumara orange-fleshed sweet potato often confused with yam.

LEEK a member of the onion family, resembles the green onion, but is much larger.

LEMON GRASS a tall, clumping, lemon-smelling and tasting, sharp-edged grass; the white lower part of the stem is used, finely chopped, in cooking.

MAPLE SYRUP a thin syrup distilled from the sap of the maple tree. Do not substitute with maple-flavoured syrup or pancake syrup.

MERGUEZ a small, spicy sausage traditionally made with lamb meat; is easily recognised because of its chilli-red colour.

MINCE MEAT also known as ground meat, as in beef, pork, lamb and veal.

MIRIN is a Japanese, champagne-coloured, cooking wine; should not be confused with sake.

MUSHROOMS
shiitake when fresh are also known as chinese black, forest or golden oak mushrooms; have an earthy taste. Are large and meaty. When dried, are known as donko or dried chinese mushrooms; rehydrate before use.

swiss brown light to dark brown mushrooms with full-bodied flavour; also known as roman or cremini. Button or cap mushrooms can be substituted.

NAAN leavened bread associated with tandoori dishes of northern India.

OKRA also known as bamia or lady fingers; a green, ridged, oblong pod with a furry skin.

ONIONS
green also known as scallion or, incorrectly, shallot; an immature onion picked before the bulb has formed.

red also known as spanish, red spanish or bermuda onion; a sweet-flavoured, large, purple-red onion.

spring crisp, narrow green-leafed tops and a round sweet white bulb larger than green onions.

OUZO a spirit with a strong aniseed flavour.

PANCETTA an Italian bacon cured in spices and salt.

PAPRIKA ground dried red capsicum; available sweet or hot.

POLENTA also known as cornmeal; a flour-like cereal made of dried corn (maize) sold ground in several different textures.

PROSCIUTTO cured, air-dried (unsmoked), pressed ham; usually thinly sliced.

PRUNES commercially or sun-dried plums.

QUAIL small (250g-300g), delicate flavoured, domestic game birds; also known as partridge.

READY-ROLLED PUFF PASTRY packaged sheets of frozen puff pastry, available from supermarkets.

REDCURRANT JELLY a preserve made from redcurrants; used as a glaze for desserts and meats or in sauces.

SAFFRON available in strands or ground form; imparts a yellow-orange colour to food. Store in the freezer.

SAKE Japan's favourite rice wine. If sake is unavailable, dry sherry, vermouth or brandy can be used as a substitute.

SAMBAL OELEK also ulek or olek; a salty paste made from ground chillies and vinegar.

SAUCES
hoison a thick, sweet and spicy Chinese paste made from salted fermented soy beans, onions and garlic.

kecap manis a dark, thick, sweet soy sauce

soy also known as sieu; made from fermented soy beans.

SHALLOTS also called french shallots, golden shallots or eschalots; small, elongated, brown-skinned members of the onion family.

SHERRY fortified wine consumed as an aperitif or used in cooking.

SICHUAN PEPPERCORNS a mildly hot spice also known as szechuan or chinese pepper. Have a distinctive peppery-lemon flavour and aroma.

SILVERBEET also known as swiss chard or chard.

SPATCHCOCK a small chicken (poussin), no more than six weeks old, weighing a maximum 500g. Also, a cooking technique where a small chicken is split open, then flattened and grilled.

SPINACH also known as english spinach and, incorrectly, silverbeet.

STAR ANISE a dried star-shaped pod whose seeds have an astringent aniseed flavour.

STOUT BEER usually darker and heavier than ale due to the colour and flavour from the roasted malt used in its production.

SUGAR
brown an extremely soft, fine granulated sugar retaining molasses for its characteristic colour and flavour.

palm light brown to black in colour and usually sold in rock-hard cakes; substitute it with brown sugar if unavailable.

SUMAC a purple-red, astringent spice that adds a tart, lemony flavour. Can be found in Middle-Eastern food stores.

TAMARIND CONCENTRATE (or paste) the distillation of tamarind juice into a condensed, compacted paste. Thick and purple-black, it is ready-to-use, with no soaking or straining.

TURKISH BREAD also known as pide.

TURMERIC also known as kamin; related to galangal and ginger. Must be grated or pounded to release its somewhat acrid aroma and pungent flavour. Fresh turmeric may be substituted with dried turmeric powder (2 teaspoons of ground turmeric plus a teaspoon of sugar for every 20g of fresh turmeric called for in a recipe).

UDON NOODLES available fresh and dried, these Japanese broad white wheat noodles are similar to the ones in homemade chicken noodle soup.

ZUCCHINI also known as courgette.

index

facts + figures

Wherever you live, you'll be able to use our recipes with the help of these easy-to-follow conversions. While these conversions are approximate only, the difference between an exact and the approximate conversion of various liquid and dry measures is minimal and will not affect your cooking results.

LIQUID MEASURES

METRIC	IMPERIAL
30ml	1 fluid oz
60ml	2 fluid oz
100ml	3 fluid oz
125ml	4 fluid oz
150ml	5 fluid oz (¼ pint/1 gill)
190ml	6 fluid oz
250ml	8 fluid oz
300ml	10 fluid oz (½ pint)
500ml	16 fluid oz
600ml	20 fluid oz (1 pint)
1000ml (1 litre)	1¾ pints

MEASURING EQUIPMENT

The difference between one country's measuring cups and another's is, at most, within a 2 or 3 teaspoon variance. (For the record, one Australian metric measuring cup holds approximately 250ml.) The most accurate way of measuring dry ingredients is to weigh them. When measuring liquids, use a clear glass or plastic jug with the metric markings. (One Australian metric tablespoon holds 20ml; one Australian metric teaspoon holds 5ml.)

DRY MEASURES

METRIC	IMPERIAL
15g	½oz
30g	1oz
60g	2oz
90g	3oz
125g	4oz (¼lb)
155g	5oz
185g	6oz
220g	7oz
250g	8oz (½lb)
280g	9oz
315g	10oz
345g	11oz
375g	12oz (¾lb)
410g	13oz
440g	14oz
470g	15oz
500g	16oz (1lb)
750g	24oz (1½lb)
1kg	32oz (2lb)

HELPFUL MEASURES

METRIC	IMPERIAL
3mm	⅛in
6mm	¼in
1cm	½in
2cm	¾in
2.5cm	1in
5cm	2in
6cm	2½in
8cm	3in
10cm	4in
13cm	5in
15cm	6in
18cm	7in
20cm	8in
23cm	9in
25cm	10in
28cm	11in
30cm	12in (1ft)

HOW TO MEASURE

When using graduated metric measuring cups, shake dry ingredients loosely into the appropriate cup. Do not tap the cup on a bench or tightly pack the ingredients unless directed to do so. Level top of measuring cups and measuring spoons with a knife. When measuring liquids, place a clear glass or plastic jug with metric markings on a flat surface to check accuracy at eye level.

Note: North America, NZ and the UK use 15ml tablespoons. All cup and spoon measurements are level.

We use large eggs having an average weight of 60g.

OVEN TEMPERATURES

These oven temperatures are only a guide. Always check the manufacturer's manual.

	°C (CELSIUS)	°F (FAHRENHEIT)	GAS MARK
Very slow	120	250	½
Slow	140-150	275-300	1-2
Moderately slow	170	325	3
Moderate	180-190	350-375	4-5
Moderately hot	200	400	6
Hot	220-230	425-450	7-8
Very hot	240	475	9

Looking after **your interest...**

Keep your ACP cookbooks clean, tidy and within easy reach with
a book cover designed to hold up to 12 books. Plus you can follow
our recipes perfectly with a set of accurate measuring cups and
spoons, as used by *The Australian Women's Weekly* Test Kitchen.

To order

Mail or fax Photocopy and complete the coupon
below and post to ACP Books Reader Offer,
ACP Publishing, GPO Box 4967,
Sydney NSW 2001, or fax to (02) 9267 4967.

Phone Have your credit card details ready,
then phone 136 116
(Mon-Fri, 8.00am-6.00pm;
Sat, 8.00am-6.00pm).

Price

Book Holder

Australia: $13.10 (incl. GST).
Elsewhere: $A21.95.

Metric Measuring Set

Australia: $6.50 (incl. GST).
New Zealand: $A8.00.
Elsewhere: $A9.95.

Prices include postage and handling.
This offer is available in all countries.

Payment

Australian residents

We accept the credit cards listed on
the coupon, money orders and cheques.

Overseas residents

We accept the credit cards listed on
the coupon, drafts in $A drawn
on an Australian bank, and
also UK, NZ and US cheques
in the currency of the country
of issue. Credit card charges
are at the exchange rate current
at the time of payment.

Photocopy and complete coupon below

- -

☐ **Book Holder**

☐ **Metric Measuring Set**
Please indicate number(s) required.

Mr/Mrs/Ms _____

Address _____

_____

Postcode _____ Country _____

Ph: Business hours ( ) _____

I enclose my cheque/money order for $ _____
payable to ACP Publishing.

OR: please charge my

☐ Bankcard ☐ Visa ☐ Mastercard

☐ Diners Club ☐ American Express

| | | | | | | | | | | | | | | | | |

Card number

Expiry date ____ /____

Cardholder's signature _____

Please allow up to 30 days delivery within Australia.
Allow up to 6 weeks for overseas deliveries.
Both offers expire 31/12/05. HLNCa05

Test Kitchen
Food director *Pamela Clark*
Food editor *Karen Hammial*
Assistant food editor *Amira Georgy*
Test Kitchen manager *Cathie Lonnie*
Home economists *Sammie Coryton,*
Nancy Duran, Nicole Jennings, Elizabeth Mac
Christina Martignago, Sharon Reeve,
Susie Riggall, Kirrily Smith, Helen Webster
Editorial coordinator *Rebecca Steyns*

ACP Books
Editorial director *Susan Tomnay*
Creative director *Hieu Chi Nguyen*
Senior editors *Wendy Bryant, Stephanie Kistr*
Designer *Jackie Richards*
Studio manager *Caryl Wiggins*
Design assistant *Josii Do*
Editorial coordinator *Merryn Pearse*
Sales director *Brian Cearnes*
Rights manager *Jane Hazell*
Marketing director *Nicole Pizanis*
Marketing manager *Katie Graham*
Brand manager *Renée Crea*
Sales and marketing coordinator *Gabrielle Bott*
Pre-press *Harry Palmer*
Production manager *Carol Currie*
Business manager *Seymour Cohen*
Business analyst *Martin Howes*
Chief executive officer *John Alexander*
Group publisher *Pat Ingram*
Publisher *Sue Wannan*
Editor-in-chief *Deborah Thomas*
Produced by ACP Books, Sydney.
Printed by Times Printers, Singapore.
Published by ACP Publishing Pty Limited,
54 Park St, Sydney; GPO Box 4088,
Sydney, NSW 2001.
Ph: (02) 9282 8618 Fax: (02) 9267 9438.
acpbooks@acp.com.au
www.acpbooks.com.au
To order books, phone 136 116.
Send recipe enquiries to:
recipeenquiries@acp.com.au
AUSTRALIA: Distributed by Network Services
GPO Box 4088, Sydney, NSW 2001.
Ph: (02) 9282 8777 Fax: (02) 9264 3278.
UNITED KINGDOM: Distributed by Australian
Consolidated Press (UK), Moulton Park
Business Centre, Red House Rd,
Moulton Park, Northampton, NN3 6AQ.
Ph: (01604) 497531 Fax: (01604) 497533
acpukltd@aol.com
CANADA: Distributed by Whitecap Books Ltd
351 Lynn Ave, North Vancouver, BC, V7J 2C4.
Ph: (604) 980 9852 Fax: (604) 980 8197
customerservice@whitecap.ca
www.whitecap.ca
NEW ZEALAND: Distributed by Netlink
Distribution Company, ACP Media Centre,
Cnr Fanshawe and Beaumont Streets,
Westhaven, Auckland.
PO Box 47906, Ponsonby, Auckland, NZ.
Ph: (09) 366 9966 ask@ndcnz.co.nz
SOUTH AFRICA: Distributed by PSD
Promotions, 30 Diesel Road Isando,
Gauteng Johannesburg.
PO Box 1175, Isando 1600, Gauteng
Johannesburg.
Ph: (2711) 392 6065/6/7
Fax: (2711) 392 6079/80
orders@psdprom.co.za

Clark, Pamela.
The Australian Women's Weekly
New casseroles.

Includes index.
ISBN 1 86396 414 2
1. Casserole cookery. I. Title.
II Title: Australian Women's Weekly

641.821
© ACP Publishing Pty Limited 2005
ABN 18 053 273 546
This publication is copyright. No part of it may be
reproduced or transmitted in any form withou
the written permission of the publishers.
The publishers would like to thank the followi
for props used in photography:
The Peppergreen Trading Store, Berrima.